Naked Wine

Naked Wine

LETTING GRAPES DO WHAT COMES NATURALLY

Alice Feiring

Da Capo Press
A MEMBER OF THE PERSEUS BOOKS GROUP

Printed in the United States of America.
For information, address Da Capo Press, 11 Cambridge Center,
Cambridge, MA 02142.

Designed by Timm Bryson
Set in 11.5 point Adobe Jenson Pro by The Perseus Books Group

Library of Congress Cataloging-in-Publication Data
Feiring, Alice.
 Naked wine : letting grapes do what comes naturally / Alice Feiring.
  p. cm.
 Includes index.
 ISBN 978-0-306-81953-7 (hardcover : alk. paper)—ISBN 978-0-306-
82048-9 (e-book)
 1. Organic wines. 2. Wine and wine making. 3. Organic viticulture. I.
Title.
 TP548.6.O74F45 2011
 641.2'2—dc23
 2011020816

Published by Da Capo Press
A Member of the Perseus Books Group
www.dacapopress.com

Da Capo Press books are available at special discounts for bulk purchases
in the U.S. by corporations, institutions, and other organizations. For
more information, please contact the Special Markets Department at the
Perseus Books Group, 2300 Chestnut Street, Suite 200, Philadelphia, PA
19103, or call (800) 810-4145, ext. 5000, or e-mail
special.markets@perseusbooks.com.

10 9 8 7 6 5 4 3 2 1

FOR

David Lett and Marcel Lapierre

The mysteries of faith are degraded if they are made into an object of affirmation and negation, when in reality they should be an object of contemplation.

—SIMONE WEIL

CONTENTS

Prologue

When it comes to wine, I can be polarizing. I don't mean to be; I just have unnaturally strong opinions. Take, for example, the supposedly provocative notion, "Why add anything to wine that isn't necessary?" Though barely five feet tall, nearly one hundred pounds, that query, out of my lips, can spark forest fires of controversy, inciting far larger people to do battle with me. Yet having resigned myself to this sad state of affairs, I persist, because as Eleanor Roosevelt said, "Do what you feel in your heart to be right, you'll be criticized for it anyway."

So when I glanced at my phone's caller ID, saw Oregon, and heard the gentleman introduce himself as Jason Lett, my first reaction was pleasure. I liked Jason, an intense man who was the son of David Lett, the founder of Oregon's edgy Eyrie Vineyard. If you handed Jason a banjo, he could be Central Casting's pick for the young Pete Seeger. But my second reaction was, *Oh no! Did I do something wrong? Did I say something careless about Eyrie on my blog? Did I somehow screw something up?*

"What's up?" I asked cautiously. That's when he propositioned me.

"I was talking to Dad. We think it's time you made your own wine. Come here. Make it exactly like you want it—all natural, nothing added, nothing taken away. Go hardcore on us. Use all the stems, no sulfur, anything!"

The Letts share many of the wine values that often get me into trouble when I shoot my mouth off about them. The elder Lett was the pioneer who, in the mid-1960s planted the first Pinot Noir in the Willamette Valley and the first Pinot Gris in America. While not whole hog into the natural-wine thing the way I am, the Letts cut close to it. On their fifty acres in the Red Hills district, they farm without insecticides or pesticides. They eschew the trendy use of irrigation and opt for dry farming. Instead of an antiseptic, hospital-like environment in their cellar, spongy black mold grows on the walls. They pay no attention to point-giving critics—who, in turn, pay little attention to them. The Letts are my kind of wine guys.

Jason proposed giving me a half ton of grapes to play with. He vowed to leave me and my fruit alone until the first fermentation—the one that converts sugar into alcohol—was completed. At that point, I was free to return home, leaving the Letts to take care of what the French call *élevage*, holding the wine while it matured and stabilized prior to bottling. They would own the wine. I could buy some, if I wished.

While I recognized this as a rare opportunity, the truth was that I never wanted to make wine. A few years back, I interviewed a California banker for a story. He posed the question "Doesn't everyone who loves wine eventually want to make it?"

My answer was no.

But I had to admit that Jason's offer was tempting. With the gauntlet thrown, my competitive side awoke. In no time at all, however, that competitive side disappeared and was replaced by a vision of me as a victim. There sat Alice, trapped in a room, while Rumpelstiltskin waited for her to turn straw into gold. If she failed, he'd swipe her first born.

"If I run into trouble," I asked, "like stuck fermentation, or if I need help getting it into the barrel, you'll be there to help me, right?"

Jason laughed. "We'll be in the middle of crush ourselves. You think we'd have time?"

I gulped. My nightmare of being locked in a room until my impossible task was completed was close to the truth.

Like a flounder in a pail, I flip-flopped with indecision. Yes? No? What to do? Oh, how to torture Alice. The specter of failure was terrifying. Sure, I didn't want to waste prime Willamette Valley fruit, but what if making wine according to my principles proved to be beyond my reach? I had been so vocal about my belief and love for wines made without any additives, what if I failed? Would the public accept my excuse that I was a writer and not a winemaker and be forgiving? My grandfather's wine turned to vinegar; so could mine. Conversely, after I stomped, the fruit could stubbornly refuse to ferment or, alternatively, might never stop fermenting. If that happened, I could be stuck in the Willamette Valley for years.

I believed that making wine without additives or industrial enological heroics was absolutely a grape's given right, but what if? . . . What if? . . . What if I had based my writing reputation on a method of winemaking more difficult than I thought it would be? I began to think that making wine in my bathtub, while not authentic, would be saner. I wasn't a complete idiot. I had plenty of vinification book knowledge. But on a practical level, I was stumped when I tried to figure out the mechanics of transferring wine from a fermentation tank to a barrel. I had no idea how I was going to press the juice from the skins. When Jason suggested I squeeze out the wine through cheesecloth, I thought he was kidding.

A month later, I had other opportunities on my mind and Jason's phone call had receded into the shadows.

CHAPTER I

Fate or Folly

Levin finished his glass and they were silent for a while.

—LEO TOLSTOY

During the summer of 2008, in the midst of a book tour, I found myself driving around California in a rental car. One of my last stops was in the Sonoma town of Healdsburg. So far, the readings and interviews had been fun, but as Healdsburg is packed with wine industry folk, I sensed that I was in for something different. I had been warned that as a mostly French-wine-drinking New Yorker, I would have to defend my recent editorial for the *Los Angeles Times*, which my editor had titled *California Wine? Down the Drain*, especially to a hall full of wine professionals. "Today's wines are overblown, over-oaked, over-priced and over-manipulated" were some of my stated, perhaps radical and unpopular, thoughts on the state's wine, which I firmly believed had lost its identity since 1990. Expecting the worst, I mused that instead of a thin summer frock, I should have worn a flak jacket.

After a scorcher of a day, the cool air had started to blow in relief from the ocean, twenty miles away, and I began getting a little buzzed about standing up in front of an audience. As someone who spends most of her days in an introverted state, fixated on a computer screen, I do enjoy the adrenalin that can kick in when I give a reading or a talk. That surge often makes me feel smarter and faster than I ordinarily think of myself. So, feeling in top form, I strolled into the library and waited on the sidelines of the stark auditorium to be introduced.

As I watched a mostly grim-faced crowd walk in, I nervously pressed my book into my lap. *Who were these folks?* I wondered. Wine people? Book people? Friend? Foe? In the rear, I recognized Patrick and his wife, Genevieve, from the blogger circuit. Friendly faces! They waved, and I waved back. Next to them was a serious, dark-haired man wearing a T-shirt emblazoned with "Robert Parker's Bitch." He looked more as if he were there for a lynching than a book reading.

After I was introduced, I was met with weak applause and started to fan through the pages, looking for the place to start. As I glanced up, I noticed a late arrival. A lanky man with a long torso and long arms that fell easily from his broad shoulders lumbered in wearing jeans and a plaid, 1950s-style, short-sleeved shirt, like something James Dean might have worn. He had a handsome, weathered farmer face, quite bony—and the kind of altogether lean look that made me want to cook him a good meal.

"I started out on Manischewitz," I began. Patrick, who is part Jewish, laughed at this remark. *God bless you*, I thought, and continued. "But by the time my father ran off after the neighbor's wife, I had moved on to Mateus."

Blank. The audience wasn't reacting.

"I was indebted to my father's mistress for one thing; she told me to raid her ex-husband's wine cellar."

This was supposed to be funny. Not to them, however. I was definitely out of my comfort zone, my shtetl. So as quickly as I could, I segued to question and answer, not realizing I was opening up the lion's cage. Mr. Parker's Bitch shot his arm in the air. "Do you regret writing that piece for the *LA Times*?"

"I got your attention with it, didn't I? It got people talking, didn't it?"

Cracking open a dialogue didn't seem to matter. But in my yeshiva training, raising the question was just as important as having the answer.

He then accused me of shameless marketing. *How?* I wondered. Merely by reading from my book? I was being accused of wanting people to know about my book and read it. Guilty as charged. But I wrote a book because I believed in my words and in the message. Of course. I wanted people to know about it and read it. I had a thought: Perhaps I should start belting out Édith Piaf's *Je ne regrette rien?*

I don't want to play the sex card, but if I were a man, would I bear the brunt of this level of hostility? It's hard to tell, but so far, my experience has told me that invective-slinging men are bound by far fewer rules of decorum than outspoken women.

Which might be why he next said, "You're no different than Parker."

"Actually, I'm quite different from the great critic," I said. "First off, I'm critical, but not a wine critic."

"Are you writing another book?" someone else asked. I thought, *Great, an easy question.*

"Yes, about high-design wine cellars," I answered, and as I did, an elderly man with a sun-baked face patted the woman's shoulder next to him, got up and left, shaking his head.

I was grateful when the kind man who looked as if he needed a good meal (and who turned out to be a local winemaker) started to dominate the conversation. "I wonder if the modern taste for sweet wine is linked to love of soda," he said. Even more interesting was to hear him, a California winemaker, muse aloud in front of his peers about the way his fellow winemakers were working. "We are such a young wine-growing community," he said, "we should simply make wine and let the results do the talking, rather than proclaim that such and such a region expresses that sense of place, referred to as terroir, in any particular way."

The woman whose elderly companion had left waved her hand. She had been looking at me in such a hard, judging way that I took a deep breath in preparation when I called on her. But instead, she talked about the man who had just left the room, her father. Her family owned vineyards, and he sometimes made wine. "Some years it's transcendent and others less so, but because I love my father, his wine is always my favorite. And with chemistry, we lose the emotion in the wine, and that's criminal."

I was very moved by her words and grateful for them. She was with me. She thought I had something to offer. At that point, I realized that most of the audience were indeed winemakers and growers, and perhaps they didn't hate me after all. Perhaps the fault was mine, and I began to think that not only did I not understand California wines, but perhaps I didn't understand Californians.

The kind man followed up by addressing the audience: "If you do something to the wine, have a well-thought-out rationale, and be prepared to talk about it. As you know, there is a lot of bullshit in the selling of wine and wine-growing and winemaking practices are often kept secret from wine drinkers. Winemakers are doing too much to the wines and are duping the public. It's time we 'fessed up and stopped."

He looked around him, to see if he was getting any support. Patrick and Genevieve were nodding their heads affirmatively, but many in the audience had their arms akimbo.

Afterward, the lanky man approached and he thanked me. I thanked him with greater enthusiasm; in fact, I felt like giving him a grateful kiss. He introduced himself as Kevin Hamel, the head winemaker for Pellegrini Family Vineyards. We lingered, and after the rest of the audience cleared away, we decided to go out for a drink. We walked to one of the swank places in town, his flip-flops clicking on the cement. Arriving at the bar, we seized the wine list. Turns out, we had the same thought, a bottle of Leroy simple Burgundy, only fifty-nine dollars. The wines that I love—the wines that I tend to buy, like that Leroy 1999—were made with very low intervention from soils that had not been chemically worked.

"Who was the hostile dude?" I asked. Happy with the Burgundy's fragrance and flavor, I started to settle down from the adrenalin rush.

"Josh. He has a blog called *Pinotblogger*, awaiting his first Pinot harvest," Kevin said, adding that he was surprised by the man's aggressive attack.

"Did I beg for it?" I asked. "Though I long to be perfectly clear and adorable, not everyone can understand me or love me."

"I thought you were terrific," he said. "That was a hard audience, and they were ready to hate you for hitting them with the hard stuff."

I admit, I'm a sucker for flattery. Kevin was intrigued by my ideas. We seemed to have similar palates, which made it easier. It always makes it easier. We talked wine. He regaled me with stories of the trade.

"You should see the tricks I see at the winery." Kevin made the wine for the Pellegrinis, but also serviced other clients, overseeing other winemaker protocols. "There's one guy in here, pretty respected winemaker. He throws the book at the wines, tannins, and enzymes. He uses the whole Scott Laboratory ingredient list. Talk to him about natural fermentations, and his hair starts to fall out of his head."

Then he told me a story about the winemaker Merry Edwards, who used to oversee the Pellegrini wines.

"The first year I was at Pellegrini," he said, "she was looking over my shoulder into the Cabernet vat and said to me, 'You threw some oak chips at it, right?' 'Um, no,' I told her. 'Oh, you guys!' she said. 'You'll never have any color or get rid of the green flavors if you don't.'"

"And did you?" I asked.

He looked at me, wounded as if to say, How could you possibly ask? This man, I thought, was a sensitive type.

For his own wine, he preferred the neutrality of old wood and never adjusted the acidity artificially or used enzymes. More recently, he had started to shun adding yeast, not only in his own label, Hamel Wines, but in Pellegrini as well, relying on what came naturally. Right then and there, we made a pact. He was going to become a soldier of the natural-wine revolution. We toasted to the future, and then he posed the question I feared. Would I taste his own wine?

I felt queasy, as if I had given a reading and a student rushed me with manuscript in hand, asking if would I read his novel. But here, I had to say yes. I had to taste his wine. There was no way around it.

We left the bar at Cyrus, and I gave him a lift to his bungalow, which was practically hidden under a brush of trees and overgrowth. Since it was a gorgeous evening, we sat out on his stoop to sip under a sky sprinkled with stars as he popped and then poured his own 2005 Pinot. Here was the dilemma. How far did I take my honesty? Too far? Would I risk offending him? But for the sake of blossoming friendship, how could I possibly base anything on a false foundation? I liked the wine enough—for a Californian wine. Then, being inimitably Alice, I asked, "Why did you tell me you didn't add yeast to it?"

He looked down at his flip-flops and said that the vintage that was presently aging up was not yeasted, but the one in my glass was. It had taken him some time to realize he didn't need to add yeast, and now he believed it made a better wine.

Even though I left for my B&B that evening without even a handshake for a good-bye, Kevin and I kept the dialogue going after I landed back in my New York City apartment and became friendlier over the next month. That's when I received in my mailbox a very amusing menu from Jason Lett. In his wonderfully quirky way, Jason delivered an invitation, reminding me of an offer that I had completely forgotten.

In this ingenious menu was a list of my winemaking options (for a copy of this menu, see Carte de Menu in the back of this book). *Why not?* I thought. Why the hell not go ahead and make wine? I had plenty of encouragement from those who thought this was a terrific opportunity. On the other hand, not everyone considered it a good idea. One of the doubters, an irascible yet lovable importer of natural wines, scolded me, "You're going to be guilty of exactly what you rail against." It was true, I have often written and spoken out about how the New World model of winemaking separated the farmer from the winemaker. "You're going to become one of those dilettante winemakers who play at making wine. Jesus, Alice," he said, disgusted.

"Oh, come on," I replied. "Give me a break!" I was looking for a shred of sympathy from this former mentor of mine. I had plenty to learn from this experiment, even if I wasn't going to be farming my own grapes first. I was a writer, not a winemaker, after all. And did this little experience make me a so-called flying winemaker, like the famous wine consultant, Michel Rolland, who flies around the world telling people how to make wine? No, of course not. This was just an adventure.

The importer hung up on me.

Dismayed, I consulted my Californian friend, Kevin. He felt exactly the opposite of how the importer felt. "You're a fool if you don't take this opportunity," he scolded me.

"But I'm terrified," I said. "This would be a public humiliation if I failed."

"That's stupid. Winemaking is merely controlled spoilage. All we do is make a big mess and then clean it up. You need to be very clean. Easy." He was playing good cop to the importer's bad.

"But I'm a dreadful slob," I responded. "Cleaning up after myself is genetically impossible. When I was growing up, my mother told me that I didn't need to learn how to clean; my maid would do it. Obviously, she never thought I'd be single, living in a five-floor walk-up with uneven floors and a bathtub in the kitchen. To this day, I am neurotic about my inability to wash the smell of fish off my plates. Somehow in my life, the maid never materialized, and deep cleaning never became a skill I excelled at."

I could tell he didn't believe me. "I'll do your fish dishes for you," he said.

"Thank you, Kevin," I said.

"Look, get over it," he said. "And you need to know how to drive a forklift. That's the most important thing. Come out here, and I'll teach you."

"To drive a forklift?" I asked. He said yes; he'd show me punch-downs, show me around the equipment, and let me see just how small a half ton of grapes was.

His offer was intriguing, and a few weeks later, I flew out to San Francisco for my remedial course in winemaking. Kevin picked me up at the airport, and we drove directly to Olivet Lane, past the old gnarly vines and the deserted Pellegrini Winery. Everyone had already gone home for the evening. We parked right on the crush pad, the area outside the corrugated steel building where the grape crushing equipment stood. Earlier that day, this was where the workers had processed about twenty tons of grapes. The air was resplendent with the smells of the first fermentation, a collection of aromas I've never been able to adequately describe. This is not a fruit smell, but more the smell of transformation.

Placed on the crush pad were a few oversized LEGO cubes. These containers were about three and a half feet tall and could each hold a half ton of grapes.

Peering into them and seeing a puny amount of crushed grapes, I shouted to Kevin, who had disappeared inside the building, "This is nothing! I can handle that many grapes sleepwalking!"

Instead of a response, I heard the whizz of a forklift sneaking up behind me. "Hop on in," Kevin said as he got out and gallantly assisted me behind the wheel of the diminutive robotic vehicle. That thing could spin on a dime, but its main talent was housed in its two front fangs that moved bins from one place to the other. I admit to feeling great power as I lifted up a bin, effortlessly, and didn't drop the precious cargo.

During the next few days, Kevin proved an amiable friend and chauffeur who willingly ferried me around to winery visits. In an offhand comment, he told me about Ridgely Evers, an olive oil mogul who sold the oil under the DaVero label and also grew Sagrantino grapes. I was surprised to hear of the existence of this grape in any quantity in California as it was a variety that lived almost exclusively in the Umbrian town of Montefalco and produced a wine I was quite fond of. Wanting to see such an oddity, I begged Kevin to take me to see the vines. We did just that on an extremely hot and dry day. The vines were in back of the Evers's house, flanked by Sangiovese vines. The poor things were suffering from the high temperature. I was impressed that anyone was motivated to grow the finicky, difficult grape in a land more celebrated for its boring (for me) Cabernet and Merlot.

During my stay, I threw my arms around California. The Greenmarkets had produce that had incredible variety and flavor. The bread and gelato were better than on the East Coast, so was the coffee. The people said hello on the streets, which was quite an adjustment. I loved the local library, too. I went to music night in the square, where the town turned out to picnic and dance. Even cute eighty-year-old couples did the two-step on the paths, in between the checkered tablecloths and makeshift spreads. The sexuality and romance that lingered into the twilight reminded me of the elderly couples who walk arm in arm in small Spanish villages for the evening stroll. Healdsburg on a clear night when Jupiter was piggybacking the moon was as sweet as the air. Everywhere around me, people were immersed in grapes, fermentation, and the vintage. People everywhere were drinking wine. For the first time, I saw just how profoundly entwined grape was in California's culture. Had I maligned this state unfairly? Was there something deeper here for me to discover? Yes, I was sure there was.

When I left, Kevin offered that if I ran into trouble in Oregon, I could always call him. He'd be the secret weapon. I was empowered. I could do this winemaking thing, naturally.

When I returned home, I called Jason to tell him that I intended to accept. The plan was to arrive in early October, when the Willamette Valley was probably going to start its vintage. But then, a mere few weeks before I was scheduled to leave for the Pacific Northwest, Jason called. He told me that this, in the end, wouldn't be the right time for the experiment. His father was seriously ill.

David Lett died early in the month, on October 9. It would have been an honor for me to experiment under his roof, getting to know the iconic David and his family better. I documented my David memories on my blog. I fondly remembered a lunch in Oregon, where David had twirled me in the aisle of the restaurant before he paraded out older vintages of his Pinot Noir and Pinot Gris. I was stunned at how the world sinfully ignored his sensual, fragrant and transparent wines. David's wines sang their own particular song of delicacy. He himself was blunt, opinionated, and profound, and yet his wines, save for their profundity, hinted at another side of the man. My own loss was small; the wine community's was far greater. Now it was up to Jason to make his mark on the fruit from his family's land. My venture into making wine in Oregon's Willamette was not meant to be.

Sensing that I had grown attached to the adventure, Kevin sent me an e-mail. "We do have grapes out in this state, too, you know," he teasingly wrote.

Well, true. But wasn't I the person who had slammed California wines, hard? Wouldn't the irony be a wee bit too much? And then, I didn't have the money to fund this project on my own. I needed an offer from someone who would give me grapes.

Kevin had some ideas. He tried to lure me with some Mendocino Carignan. He had been purchasing the fruit and vinifying it for the Pellegrini label; perhaps I could be the "consultant" winemaker on that? I am a believer in the late-ripening variety, which is fantastic from Spain and the southwest of France and is also intriguing from California. Those grapes would be ready at the end of October. The timing was perfect.

There was a problem, though. The Carignan was not farmed organically, and for me, organic farming was becoming an essential parameter. Also, I was committed to picking the fruit myself. Finally, and not inconsequentially, I would be an assistant to Kevin, demoted from being captain of my own ship, as Jason had promised. Making wine alongside Kevin would ensure I wouldn't make any dumb mistakes, but it would also compromise how much I could actually learn from the experience.

No, I recanted. California just wasn't going to work.

"What about Ridgely Evers's Sagrantino?" he asked.

Sagrantino had entered my life by a chance meeting over a bottle in 1997 during a mostly nondescript trade tasting of Italian wine in Midtown Manhattan. The wine was from Filippo Antonelli. But I had forgotten about it until I retasted it by chance the next year. Consulting my notes from the previous year, I saw that I had circled Antonelli's wine and had added a note: "Must find out more." Finally, in 2000, I did just that. I'm too attracted to drama for my own good, and this wine was a case in point. Its shockingly rough tannins with a plump, *mi-cuit* prune/plum fruit intrigued me. I found a magazine that assigned an article, and I flew to Italy. I landed in Montefalco, where the grape grows almost exclusively. The month was March, and the wheat fields in the surrounding land, deemed not suitable for grapes or olive trees, were leprechaun green. Rural, beautiful.

For most of its history, the Sagrantino was made into a sweet wine used for sacramental purposes. In the 1980s, the Montefalco winemakers started to work on perfecting a dry style, and there was no masking its sandpaper-like tannins, sun-baked fruit, and rusty-iron acidity. When I visited the area in 2000, there were fifteen producers. That number doubled in the next ten years, even though the grape is difficult to grow and to work with. As it also commands the highest prices for a dry red wine in the region, however, the big money moved in and so did the tricks, additives, and new oak.

My two favorites, then as now, sidestep brash modernity and make wine true to the grape. Filippo Antonelli's, while not an ultranatural, is respectful. His wines are both shy and elegant. Paolo Bea's son Giampiero makes the family vino and is active in the Italian natural-wine movement. His wine is chestnut, honeyed, and seductive.

So now Kevin was raising the possibility of enticing Ridgely Evers to allow the two of us to make that Sagrantino in Sonoma County, under the DaVero label. Even though I had done quite a successful job of talking myself out of the adventure, citing that there was little to interest me in Sonoma's climate and soil, I just couldn't say no. Kevin had called my bluff by meeting my need to work with organic grapes and to know where the grapes came from. But the remaining question was whether Ridgely Evers, the ultimate owner of the wine, would permit me to make a wine that was jumped into and foot-stomped and not adjusted in any way other than what the vintage gave us. I wasn't so sure.

I had first met Ridgely on the California trip when I had learned how to drive the forklift; we all had roasted in the heat, along with the vines, and talked farming. Ridgely had directed his attention to Kevin and hadn't seemed to notice me very much until the name Bea came up and I said, "I've spent some time with Giampiero." Then he was curious, very curious.

As it turned out, the Azienda Agricola Paolo Bea was Ridgely's come-to-Jesus wine. So knowing how Bea worked, I had been very surprised when Ridgely had asked me, "What yeast strain does Bea use?"

"He never adds yeast. He relies on natural fermentations," I answered.

There's a reason Ridgely is a true CEO; he doesn't miss a trick. I didn't have to worry about his allowing us to make the wine. He had already figured out how I would fit into the job. When Kevin suggested we make the wine, Ridgley probably reckoned we'd have a direct line to Bea. And if it was good enough in Montefalco, it would be good enough for Hawk Mountain, the name of the Ridgely Evers petite vineyard.

"Can we handpick?" I now asked Kevin over the phone. "I mean, I know that the grapes are usually handpicked at Ridgely's as opposed to mechanical picking elsewhere, but can I pick the grapes myself?"

Kevin promised that Ridgely had promised, and so I immediately looked at the calendar. "What are the Brix?" I asked.

Sugar is measured in Brix, and in early October, the measure was twenty. Kevin estimated that harvest would occur at the end of October.

I must have driven Kevin crazy. The poor guy was in the middle of harvest for Pellegrini, his primary gig, yet I kept on bugging him about our little project. Being close to a saint, the man took my calls to plan, talk sugar, and argue Brix and when we were going to pick.

Kevin watched the sugars. I waited by the phone. Then I got the heads-up. Sugars were up to twenty-three, which on paper was ripe enough for me, but the taste of the grapes was still bitter. But with projected fine weather, the Brix number could spike. And that is just what happened when I got the call. "The water broke," Kevin said. "Book your ticket."

The day before I departed, I got an e-mail from Ridgely: "Actually, it is hard to get examples of real Sagrantino out in California. Could you bring a few bottles?"

With a man who is generously risking a ton of his grapes with me, how could I refuse this one request, no matter how much having to check baggage makes my blood run cold? As I had an iron-clad policy of going carry-on, I tried never to take bottles with me. Obviously, I had to bend my policy. The night before I was scheduled to leave New York, I rode my bike to De-Vino on the Lower East Side to buy the 2003 Antonelli and a wine that was a new one for me—the 2004 Di Filippo.

The next morning, though, when I arrived at the airport, I was told that I was too late to check baggage. "But I have a hundred and fifty dollars' worth of wine they'll confiscate," I said.

"Sorry," the agent replied.

I was devastated and, I imagine, charmless, but I played dirty. I sweetly invoked the name of an important New York City newspaper I do work for from time to time and said this would absolutely ruin a story. Mea culpa, I was going to write some of this experience for the *New York Times*—that was true. I pressed a supervisor to feel my pain. Success. With one caveat: I was repeatedly told that there was no guarantee my bag would be on the same flight. I watched it float away on the conveyor belt, hoping for the best.

I had stuffed my wine-picking clothes, shoes, and shorts (needed for stomping grapes) into the carry-on bag that also held my computer. My gear and the computer were the most important items. If the bottles didn't make it on the flight, it was no big deal. Because of the wine-bottle fiasco, I was now quite late and had to dash for the gate like a Pamplona runner. I made it in time, and sweating, I settled into my seat on the plane. Feeling more relaxed as we made our ascent, I reached underneath the seat in front of me to grab my MacBook Air. The computer pocket felt suspiciously flat. My clothes were there, but the sleeve that held my computer was empty.

Do all my grape adventures start with disaster? The last time I had headed off to work at harvest time, mostly picking grapes at Clos Roche Blanche in the Loire Valley, I had landed at Charles de Gaulle Airport, and the airport bus had run over my luggage, missing my foot by only a few centimeters.

I was filled with panic and flagged Cindy, a tall, blonde attendant who looked like Jessica Lange. Cindy saw the situation clearly. I was going to have a heart attack if someone didn't call back to JFK to find out if a small redhead had left a gorgeous, slim computer at security. The staff did contact the airport for me, but to no avail. No one had found anything. I was a wreck.

As the hours passed by, I slowly worked on myself and my anxiety. By the time I landed five hours later, I had reached a sort of Zen state. If it was meant to be, it was meant to be. It was only money. A yoga friend had told me that what was mine could not be lost. Toward the end of the flight, I had moved into acceptance. I was another human being walking off that plane, at least an inch taller, my hair redder, and a new member of "If this is the worst, it ain't so bad" club.

We landed early, and I was shocked to see that my luggage, unlike my computer, had miraculously made the flight, bottles intact.

Then I walked to the curb to wait for the bus to the car rental when I heard a woman say, "Miss?"

I turned around to find, Cindy, the attendant who had been so concerned about my mental state during the flight. In her hands, she held something that looked like a gray cashmere sweater. Then she peeled it back, and under that sweater was the silver computer. The machine had slid out under my seat and continued under another seat, under the sweater, which had also been left on the plane. Bless her, and bless the staff at American Airlines. What was lost was found.

Ridgely told us to arrive at 7 A.M. on Thursday for picking, and Kevin's alarm roused us at 6. All was dark, and so still. In fact, Orion was still high above the town when we woke. The sun had not yet risen, but we tanked up on more coffee waiting for the pinking of the sky, and then drove the half mile to Ridgely's rolling DaVero Estate.

Olive Ridge Ranch, home to Ridgely and his wife, Colleen McGlynn, boasts grapevines, olive trees, a farmlike vegetable garden, boar, chickens, and dogs. They note on their website that they grow Meyer lemon trees, oranges, tangerines, peaches, plums, apples, pears, blackberries, quinces, figs, persimmons, pomegranates, and lavender. The farm is converting to biodynamics, a beyond-organic form of farming that pays strict attention to the lunar cycle. Driving up the lane past his house to the vines, I saw patches of rolling landscape that looked as if it had been attacked with a backhoe. "Those goddamned wild boar," Kevin said.

Tucked behind all of this was the Hawk Mountain vineyard of Sangiovese bordered by rows of Sagrantino. The field itself had plenty of dips and dives, definitely not a flattened-out, easy-to-farm plane, as so much of the California landscape seems to me.

At the lowest part of the vineyard, I found Ridgely. His two dogs were happily eating the grapes that had fallen to the ground. At work were his vineyard manager and four pickers.

"Ready to get to work?" Ridge asked and then reprimanded us for being late. But there was only about an acre of grapes to pick, barely anything at all. I chose a row of my own and started. It was fascinating to feel the difference between the grape varieties. Gamay—the grape I worked with in the Loire—was dense, with tightly packed bunches. When the season was wet, the Gamay could hide damaging rot, which needed to be snipped out. These Sagrantino bunches were loosely knit and very healthy, with a shape that reminded me of a long, swaying elephant's trunk. The grapes' skins released a stain, black as squid ink, while Gamay's pigment was more like eggplant. The fruit's pillowy flesh indicated dehydration, as it had been a warm and dry autumn. "In California," explained Kevin, always the instructing winemaker, "this is the way grapes feel at picking—soft."

I don't mean to romanticize the picking on a small estate in Europe, but I did quickly see that the work here wasn't an emotional experience; it was business. When I was in France, I picked alongside a seasonal mix of students, housewives, and retirees, each assigned to his or her own row, and the others were all very eager to show me how to best pick out the rot and how to pick perfect bunches. We were all in it together, picking for the greater good, and we all loved the final product. But the California picking crew was a Mexican team hired by the vineyard manager. Becoming part of this group was not likely.

Ridgely's workers picked everything. They were like birds of prey on a carcass, whereas I preferred to select each bunch to make sure the grapes were perfect. Sure, it was slower, but I liked the idea of preselecting in the vineyard. In fact, they were so fast coming up behind me, I feared that if I didn't get out of the way, they'd pick me.

With four pairs of hands over and above mine already on the job, I felt as necessary as a corkscrew on a screw cap. So I just gave up and, like a God-damned dilettante, talked with Ridgely and Kevin, soaking up the gorgeous morning air but feeling sad. In an hour and a half, it was all over and I walked to the container of my grapes and waited. I felt no payback in my muscles, no sense of the effort in my back. My California picking experience, instead of being meaningful, had been laughable. The puny ninety minutes consisted of a snip here and a snip there, separating the still green stalk of the pendulous fruit from the vines and tossing it into the basket.

I had gotten myself into just the situation I wished to avoid. I was not getting close enough with the process. My great wine-making caper had started off little better than working at one of those custom crush facilities becoming popular with home wine-makers who want to take their hobby professional. For that matter, my experience was hardly an improvement on urban wineries, ones I had so disparagingly written about previously. Whether these urban producers are in San Francisco, Chicago, or New York City, the members are Sunday quarterback winemakers who choose their fruit from a variety of sources, then work with a professional winemaker. Not that urban wineries were bad— to each his own—but this was not what I was after. Sure, this Sagrantino project allowed a more hands-on connection than in an urban winery, but I started to draw the analogy of accelerating into a new relationship only to find some blocks to intimacy along the road.

"Want to get going?" Kevin asked me, putting his hand on my shoulder, looking into my sad eyes through my sunglasses.

"Sure," I said, and we drove the fifteen minutes to the Pellegrini Winery, where Ridgely was to drive over the truckload of harvested Sagrantino grapes. In the car, Kevin asked what had me so pensive. I told him that I was trying to distill what seemed discordant to me about the pervasive California attitude toward winemaking. "There are just so many pieces to the puzzle," I said. "Everything is overhandled and overprocessed. Of course I couldn't pick the grapes. What had I been thinking? The pickers work for the vineyard manager directly, not for Ridgely directly. And Ridgely isn't even the winemaker. You're his winemaker, as well as Pellegrini's winemaker. No one in the Pellegrini family makes wine. Winemaking here is so . . . well, like a factory. On top of that, there's me. Clearly, I don't belong."

Kevin is a guy. He likes to solve problems. We fell into silence. I hoped he didn't take this personally. I mean, he was a born-and-bred Californian who had rarely traveled outside the country. When I then asked him where in the world he would like to make wine, he answered that he'd perhaps choose right there on the Sonoma Coast.

"Kevin," I said, "I gave you the world, and you want your own backyard. That is actually kind of sweet." Sweet, yes, and very different from my own perspective. Yet it was surprisingly nationalistic from someone like Kevin, who, while he loves California deeply, wasn't even sure if California could actually ever make truly great wine or whether the state had found its wine identity.

We turned off the main drag and drove down a little ribbon of a road to Pellegrini. While we waited at the crush pad for Ridgely the conversation moved to safer territory: how to handle the grapes.

"Stems?" he asked.

The prevailing modern winemaking wisdom is to get rid of them before fermentation. I don't agree with this fear of green stems or the belief that they add unwanted flavors and astringency, and I couldn't care less that the stems can leach color. To my particular palate, stems helped to develop structure, spice, and fragrance, especially as the wine ages. Most of my favorite northern Rhône wines and Burgundies have 50 to 100 percent stems. But Sagrantino is different. For one, the tannins are already aggressive, and the wine has proved to be one that does not age for a long time. I had asked both Filippo Antonelli and Giampiero Bea about stems. In Montefalco, stems inclusion was not traditional.

"But dry Sagrantino is so new, there is no tradition for it, right?" I asked, trying to persuade him. The stems were extremely green. The voice of experience, Kevin, outvoted me.

"What else shall we do?" he asked.

I pulled out and read aloud the e-mail that Bea had sent me when I first had asked his advice:

> Have faith in wine and nature. Stay away from the idea of trying to dominate nature through science. When there is love for what you have in your head (and I am talking about LOVE, that sentiment that comes from the heart, as far as we are concerned, and not from GREED), the rest will come by itself!

"That's what we'll do," Kevin said just as Ridgely arrived in his truck with his two dogs, Django and Boswell, and the ton and a half of fruit, triple the amount I would have worked with at Eyrie. Bob Pellegrini, Dan Fitzgerald (Kevin's assistant), and assorted other helpers emerged from the winery and swarmed around like fruit flies. They showed the kind of curiosity one would have about a talking frog. No one had seen this grape before. Bob Pellegrini sampled a berry and laughed with great surprise. "Wow, that is tannic," he said.

In a flash, the action began. Dan (and not me) hopped into a forklift and started to drop the grapes into the de-stemmer—a long conveyor belt that sent grapes up to a machine that, with centipede-like fingers, would separate the stems from the berries. As the grapes made their way up, we plucked out grapes that looked substandard.

"What's the plan?" Ridgely asked.

"Stomp them up," Kevin answered, in his Northern California clip, "and let them turn themselves into wine."

CHAPTER 2

The Principle of Nature

In nature, nothing is perfect and everything is perfect. Trees can be contorted, bent in weird ways, and they're still beautiful.

—ALICE WALKER

To go ahead with my foolish idea of making Sagrantino in California, I had to do it as Jason Lett had suggested, according to my "principles."

Yet I was queasy with placing too much emphasis on *principle*. How one treated a wine was not a moral issue, after all. Wine in a vat was not the same as a chicken cooped up in its cage. Wine was not a goose being force-fed to fatten its liver. I didn't intend to strike up a debate about the "piety" in a wine's source, as in Michael Pollan's *Omnivore's Dilemma* or Eric Schlosser's *Fast Food Nation: The Dark Side of the All-American Meal.* I liked my wine free-range, but still, a bottle of Pineau d'Aunis couldn't stare me in the eyes and lick my face, and if I abused a Gamay grape, its drinker wouldn't scream in horror. Still, when a wine has been manipulated, I, as the drinker, *would* scream or at least decline the wine and reach for a reliable alternative, like gin or scotch.

I came to my so-called principles because the wines I enjoyed the most were made under a guiding philosophy based on nothing added and nothing taken away. This actually sounds like a delicious ideal, yet the relevance of the ideal, and the wines, seems to be endlessly debated.

"Natural" wine has been going on strong in France since the late 1970s, but from the way journalists, bloggers, and winemakers are carrying on, you would think that at best, *natural wine* was a brand-new concept and, at worst, a new link to Al Qaeda. The word *natural* itself is under fire. As Michael Pollan told me, the term is "perceived as meaningless hype from the 1970s . . . co-opted and reinterpreted. Back then, anything—even something with artificial flavors—was called natural."

Annoyingly, this accurate observation requires the consumer to be a hypervigilant ingredient reader as well as an expert at understanding spin and marketing subtext. Unquestionably, however, the "natural" food movement, flawed word and all, revolutionized the way we eat and increased the availability of organic food and other more wholesome, less-tampered-with food.

In his 1989 book, *Appetite for Change: How the Counterculture Took On the Food Industry*, food activist Warren Belasco wrote that back in the 1970s, natural food was seen as a dangerous concept that could seduce the public into romantic antimodernism, undoing many years of propaganda on the behalf of technological food production and processing.

One of the criticisms bandied about at those (like me) who love "natural" wines is that we were seduced *only* by romantic notions of wine. Somehow critics felt we were seduced by concept, not taste.

When the multibillion-dollar agribusiness came to realize that organic foods posed a threat, the industry struck back by trying to discredit organic farming. (Later, of course, agribusiness gave up this strategy and started to buy up organic businesses so that it wouldn't lose out on customers.) Belasco cited Jim Hightower, who wrote that in 1975, the $500 million organic foods business posed no immediate competitive threat to the $160 billion food industry, but that the existence of naturally produced alternatives might cause some to wonder about all of the brand names they were buying.

This is directly analogous to wine and wine buyers. One Little Falls, New Jersey, collector I wrote about had a cellar full of expensive wines he had bought on the merit of their high scores. One day, he rebelled. Quite on his own, he found natural wine. All of the sudden, he—a sixty-something-year-old who loves Italian wines—dumped the confabulated culprits, donating some to charities and selling some others off at auction. He started to hunt down Cappellanos, Occhipintis, Radikons, wines made in *ánforas* (Spanish for amphorae), wines made with no sulfur. If this situation ever happened on a large scale, the big brands could be in quite a pickle and panic to find buyers, especially at the high end.

Yet companies that provide the wine industry with wine additives—companies like Lallemand and Scott Laboratories—haven't as yet been part of the debate. They are busy addressing the need for some "natural" kinds of yeasts and organic adjuncts instead. Some of the reaction against natural-wine advocates is being generated by winemakers who could be threatened by a change in the winemaking paradigm. The anti-natural attitude is further encouraged by the world's most famous wine critic. In one restaurant review, he praised a Philadelphia restaurant because there was no "precious sommelier trying to sell us some teeth-enamel-removing wine with acid levels close to toxic, made by some sheep farmer in the north. . . . [W]e all know the type—saving the world from drinking good wine in the name of 'vinofreakism.'" The critic's sarcasm insulates the industry from serious debate about the effect that the natural-wine movement will have on the establishment.

As Pollan explained, another reverberation from the early food movement of the 1970s was the argument that everything on earth is natural. Belasco addressed this claim:

> If everything was natural, then nothing was artificial. . . . First, in agriculture, "nature" meant plagues, pestilence, and famine. The defenders of high-tech agribusiness wrongly equated "organic" with laissez-faire and somberly warned of the dire consequences of "doing nothing" and "leaving everything up to nature."

Once again, this is a page from the book of the current wine situation. A rather tired, but seemingly favorite straw-man argument gets bandied about with regularity by pundits who play with the absurd: Only wine without any intervention is "natural." One *Wine Spectator* writer accusingly said to me, "Why not only make wine from wild grapes?" Fermentation can indeed happen inside of a grape unattended. The idea of making wine from wild grapes is actually appealing, but you'd probably get a thimble full. Wine needs humans. How far human intervention goes is what is debated.

Eric Asimov of the *New York Times* observed that the world of natural wines is one of the wine world's great "hornets' nests," pointing out how "even defining the term incites the sort of Talmudic bickering usually reserved for philosophers and sports talk-radio hosts." The *San Francisco Chronicle* wrote how easily the word is corrupted. The *Chronicle*'s wine writer, Jon Bonné, had come across a note describing how one winemaker was "elevating the quality of the grapes through the most natural means possible, through a constant experimentation with clones, yeasts, barrel styles and blending of wines from various lots and barrels."

Personally, I think the word *natural* can be useful. The public needs a general word to indicate the kind of wine it is looking for, and *natural* is a natural and, while not perfect, is good enough. Until a different word is grandfathered in, like *pure*, *naked*, *real*, or even *plain*, it helps the public make distinctions between products. The danger lurks in the word's being legislature resistant and therefore easily commandeered by commercial wineries looking to keep their market share. Probably the strongest argument against using the word *natural* comes from the U.S. government's strange use of the term. The U.S. Alcohol and Tobacco Tax and Trade Bureau (TTB) uses this definition, current as of April 2011, for "natural wine": "The product of the juice or must of sound, ripe grapes or other sound, ripe fruit (including berries) made with any cellar treatment authorized." Some of the treatments allowed are the additions of water, sugar, concentrated fruit juice from the same kind of fruit, malolactic bacteria, yeast, sterilizing agents, precipitating agents, and other approved fermentation adjuncts. (See the back of the book for approved additives or processes.)

Currently, the TTB is considering the inclusion of an ingredient list, but only for nutritional value, carbohydrates, and calories. I have not been successful in getting the TTB's spokesperson, Thomas Hogue, to take my inquiry about a real ingredient list seriously enough to get a satisfactory reply. Unless winemakers start to include wine ingredients and processes on the label, I am afraid that nothing can safeguard the product. It will be up to the buyers to beware or to be guided by their taste buds.

Ridgely Evers was a small wine producer. Tiny. And even though he allowed me to make a wine generally according to my "principles," I could push natural just so far. While I could take any risk for myself, I had to keep in mind that he needed to produce a wine he could bring to market. After all, it was Ridgely who kept on reminding me of another meaning of sustainable. "Sustainable means sustainable for the farmer," or, in other words, the farmer needs to make a living.

If I had enjoyed total control—if I had been conducting my venture at the Letts' Eyrie vineyard and winery—I might have tried to make the wine differently. I'd more likely have kept the stems on instead of removing them. I would have trod the grapes once a day instead of twice. Perhaps I would have gone hardcore and left out sulfur altogether.

But the focus on sulfur, and often the arguments surrounding it (that wines without sulfur are unsound, that even the Romans knew that sulfur was needed, that it's a natural substance, etc.), often deflect greater issues: Making wine naturally is so much more complicated than that. So, yes, those old principles I supposedly had, did they have roots, I wondered, in the very beginning of winemaking itself?

I could argue that after the flood, grapes turned into wine overnight and Noah kicked off the natural-wine movement and (ever since) consumers, merchants, and makers have been trying to corrupt it. Or, to quote wine critic Robert M. Parker Jr., "Once the bean counters take charge, it's all over." He was spot on. The struggle between commerce and artisan is historic—it's human nature to mess around with commercial goods. One ancient trick (illegal yet still going on today) is adding grapes from one region to wine produced elsewhere. Just look at the Brunello di Montalcino scandal of 2003. That year, shipments of more than five notable producers were withdrawn from the market because of illegal additions in this pricey, elite wine. This is an old story. The wines from the south of Italy had been added to Barolo. Syrah from the northern Rhône had been used to bolster Bordeaux.

Wines have been tampered with since the Romans and greatly so since the medieval era. There are references to wines from France being "concocted" in England by bolstering the juice with starch, gum sugar, and "essence." Other tasty preparations included mixtures of wine dregs, vinegar, and oil, while color was altered with juice or dye. In *The Englishman's Food: A History of Five Centuries of English Diet* (published in 1958), J. C. Drummond and Anne Wilbraham refer to a tampered-wine incident recorded in an old book, *The Dictionary of Merchandise*. Merchant John Penroe was found guilty in London in 1350 for selling "unsound" wine. Penroe was sentenced to drink his own wine, have the rest poured over his head, and leave the business. Drummond and Wilbraham also describe the 1419 case of William Horold, who was pilloried "for that he falsly and devyvably gummyd and raysyd two buttes with divers fummes and unholsome other thyhnges for mannys body, and feld hem ful of old feble Spaynnissh wyn, to have a lykly manere taste and sell to the drynkyng of Romeny."

In the late 1800s, Louis Pasteur studied fermentation science, identified yeast as an agent of fermentations, and set the stage for winemaking to become more of a controlled art. His research gave both the business and artisanal sides of winemaking the tools for better fine wines and industrial wines. Yet, both types of winemaking had great setbacks because France—and then the rest of

the world—was in the throes of the vine-destroying louse phylloxera, which soon decimated the vineyards of Europe.

During this epidemic, remedies to salvage the taste of wine
sprung up. In the late 1880s, J.-F. Audibert wrote a book titled *L'art
de faire les vins d'imitation*. According to economic historian Carlo
M. Cipolla, this book was reprinted ten times and granted a medal
by the French ministry of agriculture and commerce. In Audibert's
book, there are three hundred recipes for making anything from
Château Lafite to Chambertin. The key was to use raisins, cheap
wine from the south, and chemical additives.

On a more nefarious and dangerous note, lead, diethylene glycol, and methanol have, over the years, been added to wine to increase sweetness and alcohol content. Such practices are not just
a relic of the medieval or phylloxera eras, but have been a scourge
as recently as 1985. That year, Austria was involved in a scandal
in which Austrian winemakers were adding diethylene glycol to
make their wines taste sweeter and more full bodied. A similar incident occurred in Italy a year later. The good news is that Austria
responded with much stricter wine laws and is highly unlikely to
be blackballed for bad behavior in the near future. China, however,
is a different story. While nothing lethal has been found in its
wines, nearly thirty wineries were shut down in Hebei Province
in late 2010, after the discovery that some Hebei wines contained
only 20 percent grape juice. The rest of the "wines" were pumped
up with added water, unidentified chemicals, and color additives
as well as the commonplace citric and tartaric acids.

A 2008 study conducted by the Pesticide Action Network Europe (PAN Europe), a pressure group featuring members from
France, Austria, and Germany, showed that twenty-four pesticide
contaminants, including five classified as carcinogenic, mutagenic,

reprotoxic, or endocrine interactive, showed up in over 75 ₁
of their samples. (Out of the six organic wines studied, only on﹀
had contamination.) A press release by the organization summa-
rized the study's findings: "The presence of pesticides in European
wines is a growing problem. Many grape farmers are abandoning
traditional methods of pest control in favour of using hazardous
synthetic pesticides."

This study alone should make consumers seek wines that are
natural from the ground up. And what about the additives actually
allowed in today's wines? No, they won't kill you, though I have
my suspicions that more people are allergic to added enzymes and
tannins than to modest amounts of sulfur. Recipes not so different
from Audibert's collection abound today, including the addition
of enzymes and oak chips, and processes like reverse osmosis and
thermovinification. Thermovinification, a hot maceration technique that can produce a wine in a few hours rather than a few
weeks or months, is used in many wine-producing regions. Stu-
pefyingly, in a world favoring slow food, few seem to mind fast
wine.

Counterfeit wines, phony wines with fancy labels, such as
Petrus 1982, are wreaking havoc with the auction world. The more
things change, the more things stay the same. Man's nature is con-
sistent. But I recall the words of the late and very great Barolo
winemaker, Baldo Cappellano, "The more there's fake, the more
there's need for real."

In any dark hour, an underbelly of needed authenticity arises,
and that is most probably why the birth of the current movement
lay down its roots in the late 1970s, all mixed up with the desire
for real taste, linked with seeking out honest viticulture. The nas-
cent trend didn't have a name; it was merely an exploration that

undoubtedly began with the curious scientist and vigneron from Chapelle-de-Guinchay, Jules Chauvet.

Jules Chauvet was a bachelor, a scientist, a winemaker, an obsessive, and, to some, a natural wine saint. In the black-and-white photographs of his era, he looks so "of a time": horn-rimmed glasses, button-down sweater tucked into his high-waisted pants, and, always, a tie. An immaculate man, his shoes polished to a military sheen, he was born in 1907 to a Beaujolais wine family. He pursued science and wine until his death in 1989 and wrote several technical books. He was known for his studies on carbonic maceration, the type of fermentation common in his area of Beaujolais. Carbonic maceration is an enzymatic sort of fermentation, inside the grape, instead of being yeast activated. The method involves placing the entire grape clusters in a carbon-dioxide-filled vat that is then sealed up, creating an anaerobic environment. The fermentation starts internally and bursts the berries as sugar converts to alcohol.

Little has been written about Chauvet, save for one heartwarming interview conducted in 1981 and documented in Hans Ulrich Kesselring's *Le vin en question*. I have a well-worn copy that I frequently reread. But when I came upon one of Chauvet's statements— "Wine must be naked"—I stopped. *Naked* seemed to the point; there is something exposed, vulnerable yet true.

One night, with the complement of a touch of scotch in a fragile glass with red hearts, I found one of the rare English-language references to Chauvet in print. I was reading Kermit Lynch's *Adventures on the Wine Route*. In it, the California wine importer tells the compelling story of his meeting with Chauvet.

In 1984, Lynch was in Beaujolais, looking for an authentic example of the eponymous wines. By that time, the Beaujolais region's wine had been dumbed down into the worst plonk. It was banana-driven, sickly sweet, and pumped full of sulfur. Beaujolais Nouveau had overtaken the region. In search of the old-fashioned good stuff, Lynch followed the trail of wines from the best of ten villages: Régnié, St. Amour, Chénas, Chiroubles, Juliénas, Côte de Brouilly, Brouilly, Fleurie, Moulin-à-Vent, and Morgon. He ended up at Chez Chauvet. Apocryphal stories of the man ran rampant. One story had it that Charles de Gaulle was a fan of the scientist's wines.

So was Lynch when he tasted them. The wines were in direct contrast to everything else he had sipped from the region. He believed the wine to have been made with no added sulfur or anything else, and he described them like this:

> Pale in color, with a light, pretty perfume. There were reminders of flowers, grapes and fruits like peach and apricot. It was all quite delicate from start to finish, but lively at the same time, and the flavor was elusive: more than anything, it perfumed the palate, 11 degrees in alcohol. I never tasted anything like it. It was cornucopian in its fruitiness. Yeah, cherries and berries, but peachy and apricots too and on and on. You couldn't single anything out. It was Cornucopian.

During this meeting, a perplexed Lynch asked Chauvet what had happened to the region's wines. How could a wine that could be so beautifully expressive have been so dumbed down? How could this *real* taste have been lost?

Chauvet replied with the following story. Beaujolais was always a low-alcohol wine, but the vintages of 1945 and 1947 were very hot and the grapes got quite ripe, which translated into higher alcohol: above 13 percent. The wine sold well. Eager to make big wines that most people liked, producers decided to continue to boost the alcohol by excessive chaptalization, the process of adding sugar to lengthen the fermentation time and to increase the alcohol and corpulence. Chaptalization had often been employed as needed, but now it was being used for a different purpose in the market.

Further change came in the form of technology. In the 1960s, chemical farming became fashionable. By the 1970s, most people had converted over to chemicals and synthetics in the vineyard. Once-vibrant soil became devoid of life and nutrients, inspiring the now-almost-cliché expression "There was more life in the Sahara than in the vineyards of France." You are what you eat, even if you are a grape.

Quality suffered—huge crops and low quality. Slowly, the wine's fine nature was corrupted. The coup de grâce was the rise of the marketing concept called Beaujolais Nouveau. Wine was rushed to the market by November, and insipid plonk became synonymous with Gamay. The industrial yeast 71B became commonplace, producing aromas of banana. This momentarily saved the necks of many farmers and winemakers desperate to sell their wine. They were caught between two areas that had greater acclaim, the northern Rhône and the Côte d'Or. Producers made adjustments, and soon, Beaujolais no longer deserved any respect. The region, capable of such greatness, became the vinous equivalent of candy corn, consumed only once a year. Memories were short. People in the Beaujolais region are more inclined to drink Rhône wines; no one remembered the Cru Beaujolais as the gorgeous wine it once was.

But there was finally good news. Resurrection had ridden into town.

In 1978, a young Morgon winemaker named Marcel Lapierre came to terms with the reality that he couldn't stand to drink his own wine. This was also the time when organic growing and eating started to creep into the mainstream. Lapierre experimented with no-sulfur winemaking that year. Hearing that a man of science and wine, Chauvet, was working without the substance, Lapierre sought him out. With Chauvet's help and that of Jacques Néauport, Chauvet's assistant and student-disciple, Lapierre started to change his approach to growing grapes and turning them into wine.

Like most rural Beaujolais towns, Morgon is tiny, and word spread fast. Lapierre influenced like-minded friends, most notably Max Breton (Le P'tit Max), Jean Foillard, and Jean Thévenet. They became a band, the Gang of Four. There was also another vigneron, Joseph Chamonard, a beloved old man who always worked as his elders had; in other words, he never used chemicals in the vineyard or enological tricks in his wine. He was grandfathered in, as a fifth. I view him as their mascot.

Except for the Chamonard, Lynch brought all these wines to the United States. Very quietly they started to sell, although it took a few decades for these wines to have their "immediate" impact.

Because of the reputation of Beaujolais Nouveau, Gamay from the area, even the great stuff, was a hard sell. The wine was not considered sexy; the grape not considered important. At the time, no one used the now-compelling buzzword *vin naturel*. So, there was no marketing hook. And if there was, no one would have cared. There was, however, word of mouth, and Morgon became the source of this mysterious *vin sans soufre*, wine made without added sugar, sulfur, or yeast. Soon, some more vineyards shifted back to organic. This wine movement flowed over to other areas in the Beaujolais, throughout France, and, thirty plus years later, to Italy, to Spain, and, finally, to the United States.

When it comes down to it, most roads to French natural producers lead to either Chauvet, Lapierre, or, as I would later find out, that assistant who worked with Chauvet for two years, Jacques Néauport.

I have spent a decade or so attending tastings in France. People there look familiar to me. I had often seen a handsome man with his smart head of white hair and round, blonde horn glasses at the alternate (often called "off" because they are off-site of the conventional ones) tastings in France and Europe. This man, François Morel, was the editor of *Le Rouge et le Blanc*, a journal devoted to independent winemakers, and the author of *Le vin au naturel*.

Now, sipping my second espresso, I found myself waiting for him on a clear Paris morning at Café des Musées in the Marais. He walked in, unselfconsciously chewing gum. I only recently found out that he had been at the natural-wine movement's beginning. Natural wine was his Woodstock. He looked at me carefully, and then he said, "Yes, I do know you." Funny how you can see someone for years and know nothing about him. For example, I had no idea that he had started the first natural-wine bar, called Bistrot des Envierges.

"Before we go on," he said, "we first must agree on the word *natural*."

"So the term is as controversial in France as in the United States?" I observed.

He rolled his eyes, as if to say, you have no idea. He was wrong. I did indeed know how intense the controversy could be.

I asked, "So, what is it to you?"

"To me," he said, "natural wine is without artifice. You see, that's why my book is *Le vin au naturel*, not *Vin naturel*." I love the French emphasis on the simple twist of language, yet so meaningful, yet so difficult.

When I asked him how he became involved in the natural-wine scene, he told me that he had been a writer at an art book publisher, Larousse. "I was fed up. I opened up a wine bar in the twentieth arrondissement. I had a petite amie, a girlfriend, from the Mâconnais. She asked me why I didn't have any Beaujolais in the bar. I told her there weren't any that I liked. That started it. She took me to—"

"Don't tell me," I said. "Marcel Lapierre?"

"Exactly."

François started out with his wine bar in 1985 and fell for the Mâconnais woman in 1989, just around the time the group of winemakers was being imported by Lynch—just when Chauvet died and when Néauport's influence was greatest. The girlfriend introduced him to Marcel Lapierre, and as if meeting Lapierre weren't influential enough, François actually loved the wine. One sip of the natural stuff often changes your attitude toward wine forever and often fills your life with (forgive me for saying it) meaning. François told me how the natural-winemaking philosophy from Beaujolais spread. His wine bar provided a marketplace and a market for these kinds of wines. He also added, "I would encourage winemakers to try to make wines in this other way."

All through this interview, there was the rumble of gear-shifting motorcycles—the café was open on two sides—and it was deafening.

"That was a key moment," he said. "Up until this moment, vignerons had been focused on the cellar, but now there was a shift to the vineyard. That is the meaning of natural . . . the continuation of natural into the vineyard. If the vineyard is covered with chemicals, it's not going to work; it's not natural."

It occurred to me that in today's arguments about natural wine, the strong link to organic or chemical-free vineyards is often addressed as an aside instead of the starting point. Dealing with healthy and vibrant soil is one of the key tenets. In theory, a natural wine needs to start with the soil first, and then we can talk about nothing added or taken away so that there's no masking of the natural expression of grape, place, and winemaker.

"What do you think, François?" I asked. "Is it merely an ideal? Can it be done?"

"I think what the vignerons think. If you work without sulfur, the grapes and the juice must be perfect; it's not possible in every vintage. It's the ideal. It's something you work towards."

In this way, it seems to me the natural-wine movement is classically French. What I love about the country is that ideas and argument can still be important.

Three espressos later, I figured it was time to let François go, to get on with the day. But I had one last question. After all, he had a perspective of fifteen years more than I had. "How," I asked, "did the world of vin naturel change?"

He didn't have to think long about this answer; he was ready. "Now, it's a commercial category!" he said. "There is *bio* (organic) in the supermarket. Outside of that, the fashion is in favor of those who make natural wine, yet thirty years ago, these people were seen like crazy people."

Or as James Suckling, a former writer for *Wine Spectator*, a magazine that had ignored the existence of these wines, tweeted to the world in 2010, "No longer for smelly, Birkenstock wearing hippies." Natural had officially become trendy.

François sighed and rocked his chair back on its two hind legs. "That is the contemporary misery in general, no? That is the malaise of the word *commercial*. As soon as you understand this is a way to make money, things change. Look at the Chablis wine-maker Jean-Marc Brocard. He is in biodynamics? How is this possible? And then you taste the wine, and that's the point. When you taste it, you can't hide. You can't fake it."

But they try and they will try. Many winemakers might decide against the enzymes and tannins, but the yeast and the sulfur will be sticking points.

When I visited the Louis Pasteur museum in Arbois, I found myself transfixed by the gentle daffodil color of sulfur. So beautiful, so devilish. Elemental sulfur is produced by volcanoes and is a by-product of various industrial processes. Since coal and petroleum often contain sulfur compounds, their combustion generates sulfur dioxide unless the sulfur compounds are removed before burning the fuel. Sulfur has been purportedly used since Roman times, when candles were burned in barrels to preserve wine's freshness. The sulfur binds with two oxygen molecules and becomes sulfur dioxide.

Elements, substances that are made up of only one kind of atom, are, obviously, found in nature and are therefore natural. Sulfur is natural, and for that matter, so is arsenic and plutonium, but who wants those in their wine? Unlike the latter two, small amounts of sulfur can be beneficial. It helps get rid of bad bugs in the intestines and can knock them out in wine as well. Adding a touch of sulfur is just what is needed to offer protection from spoilage by bacteria and oxidation, and it keeps volatility (that smell of nail-polish remover in wine that can signal trouble) in line.

Sulfur, in its pure form, can be dusted or sprayed on grapevines during the growing season to prevent rot and mildew. When sulfur bonds with oxygen, it forms the controversial sulfur dioxide, yet sulfur dioxide is a natural product of fermentation, present naturally at concentrations of up to 10 milligrams per liter, or 10 parts per million (ppm). For conventional wines, the amount of sulfur allowed in the United States (350 ppm) is higher than in the European Union (160 ppm for dry red wines and 210 ppm for dry white and rosé wines). As of 2011, U.S. wines labeled 100 percent organic cannot have any added sulfur. In the European Union, where there is no organic *wine* category and only wine from organic grapes, a concentration of 100 ppm is allowed. While 100 ppm is clearly lower than that in conventional wines, in the natural-wine world, the dosage would be considered so high as to provoke sneers. The natural proponents would call such a product not only a sulfured wine, but a highly sulfured one. In fact, with those high dosages, you can't even dream of making a so-called natural wine.

Sulfur needs to be handled with respect. First of all, it's terribly toxic. An excess of the substance gives a wine a nasty burn and sometimes a skunky or flinty smell. People who add a lot of sulfur to wines (e.g., the Germans, especially for their white wines that are meant to be long-lived), argue that sulfur dissipates. Those on the low- or no-sulfur side of the argument, even in Germany, would prefer to have a wine evolved in five to ten years instead of thirty and have a wine of more life. Too little sulfur, the naysayers argue, turns a wine brown just as a fresh-cut apple quickly darkens. Sulfur, or low additions of it, was the victim of possibly wrong accusations for premature oxidation of the 1996 white Burgundies. Paul Draper, who gave the world Ridge Winery in the Santa Cruz Mountains, has another take on the subject. He says that not only is sulfur beneficial to health, but it alone can bring terroir into focus. This is directly opposed to those I've met who believe a wine without sulfur is the true expression of place and grape.

Although sulfur is used as some form of liquid, sodium metabisulfite is added to the wine in safer-to-handle tablet form. I love this quote from Wikipedia: "Campden tablets [sodium or potassium metabisulfite] are also used towards the end of the fermentation process to halt the ferment before all the available sugars are converted by the yeast, hence controlling the amount of residual sweetness in the final product. This balancing between sweet, dry and tart flavors is part of the artistry of wine and cider making."

If you are a *terroirist*—a believer in terroir—and most *vin naturel* winemakers are, you have a firm belief that the DNA is written in the yeast from the vineyards. So, don't mess with the sulfur. In his interview in *Le vin en question*, Chauvet told his interviewer, "Sulfur is a poison. It poisons both the yeast and bacteria."

Then, of course, there are the health considerations of sulfur: Overdosing the wines can cause headaches and, in some people, severe reactions. Inhaling sulfur dioxide is associated with increased respiratory symptoms and disease, difficulty in breathing, and premature death. I've yet to find the winemaker who says, "Man, I just love to handle that stuff."

Transplanted Israeli Gideon Bienstock, one of the few Californian winemakers who farm the land that produces their grapes, told me a story about a winemaker who almost killed himself when adding liquid sulfur. "He jumped off the tank, forgetting how high up he was. When you're in the presence of sulfur, you just want to get the hell out of there." Now, Gideon adds a little bit when the grapes come in and then nothing, even at bottling.

Chauvet's lifetime study was carbonic maceration. Along the way, he saw that when the harvest was sound, using sulfur in the closed environment was totally pointless. Simply put, he worked very carefully, cleanly, with healthy, whole grapes, without additions, without adding yeast. Yet danger still existed. Whole-cluster fermentation in a closed vat reduced the acidity and raised a wine's pH, making the wine less stable and more susceptible to the *piqûre lactique*, the dreaded condition that is caused by a lactic-acid-producing bacillus and that can stop a wine in its tracks. It was not yet clear to me whether the practice of carbonic maceration under very cold temperatures, by refrigeration as well as layering dry ice into the vat, was perpetuated by Jules Chauvet or his assistant, Jacques Néauport. Nevertheless, the hope was that it kept the threat of lactobacillus in check, prevented the fermentation temperature from climbing dangerously high, and had the added benefit of promoting intense aromatics, which were more profound than the wine's structure would ordinarily have allowed. Chauvet loved perfume in his wine, and the lighter, quaffable aromatic became a signature for a kind of *vin naturel*. His wine also could have a bit of a spritz from the ensuing carbon dioxide gas trapped in the wine; instead of sulfur, the carbon dioxide acted as a preservative.

The desire to make wine completely without sulfur is the tipping point between the hardcore and the "natural enough" crowd. These two are the Weather Underground Organization versus the SDS (Students for a Democratic Society): both had the same goal, yet each took different paths.

By the time Chauvet died in 1989, the movement, based on unsulfured wine, was rapidly gaining enthusiastic drinkers and vintners. The group of winemakers who had their wines served at François Morel's wine bar persuaded him to host unsulfured-wine tastings. He did this once a year until he shuttered his wine bar in 1998. The next year, the baton for hosting the tasting was picked up by a group in the Loire, specifically, by Pierre and Catherine Breton. The Bretons worked in the region of Bourgueil, which is where the La Dive Bouteille debuted. The Dive became a think tank of sorts for this kind of winemaking. These were pre-social-media days, but in this way, when each member of the group invited a friend from another region to join the tasting, a *copinage* (about friends and sometimes about nepotism) system went viral. It was at the 2001 Dive that I made my own debut to the natural-wine world. In its madhouse energy (sort of like a Cirque du Soleil of tastings), I felt at home. I had hooked up with a friend, Joe Dressner, the first wine importer in the United States to focus on these kinds of wines, and I had also met Jenny Lefcourt. She was just starting out in the wine business and Jenny & François was about to be the second New York City–based importer of natural wines. There on the list of winemakers I saw Clos du Tue-Boeuf, a joke on Duboeuf (Georges), and Thierry Puzelat, the Loire wine producer with whom I had some history.

In the late 1990s, I had a brief and unsuccessful stint as a wine salesperson for the Puzelat brothers' first importer. Victor Schwartz, the owner of the importing house, presented the wines to me to taste, wondering if he should bring them in. "This guy is a rock star over in France," he said. I didn't know what to make of the wines, but I—not knowing anything about sulfur or natural—thought they, the Gamays and the Sauvignons, were unlike anything I had ever tasted and were delicious. He subsequently dropped them, and I left my sales job to pursue wine writing. I am not sure if the two actions were related.

I have stayed in touch with the Puzelats, and I recently asked Thierry how he came into this specific world of *vin naturel*. Again, all roads led to Marcel Lapierre.

"I started to work at the Bandol domaine, La Tour du Bon in 1990," he said. "I was introduced to Jacques Néauport in early 1991 [and he] brought me to a party at Marcel Lapierre's in July of that year. That moment was a revelation for both the life in wines I tasted and for the way of life they had."

After Thierry left La Tour du Bon in 1994, he and his brother Jean-Marie took over the family domaine, Clos du Tue-Boeuf. "Jacques came to Tue-Boeuf twice a year to taste and help us. We couldn't pay him, other than a few cases of wine. Pierre and Catherine Breton were the only other non-sulfite winemakers in the Loire in that period. Jacques was visiting them, too. There were few customers for that kind of wine back then, except three or four wine bars in Paris." Thierry had many bottles returned in the first five or six years of working that way, and I remember Victor bitching in New York about the wine's instability. Wines made without sulfur need certain care and shipping and storage under cool conditions, but it took a while for the vignerons as well as the importers responsible for shipping the bottles to figure that out.

"Anyway, I stopped with Jacques," Thierry added.

"Why?" I asked. I was starting to get very curious about this Néauport character.

"We once had a phone conversation about winemaking. He was upset and did not answer anymore. I sent him a letter, and he never answered."

More intrigue about this Jacques character, I thought.

Around 2000, the category of *sans soufre* wine exploded. Sometimes literally. What was inside the bottle could be quite unstable if rushed to market or stored on wine shelves without proper cool temperature, which often happened. Yet, it was also a time of explosive, wine-related creativity and energy. It was as much a revolution as any other cultural revolution, certainly as much as the food revolution that happened on American shores starting with Alice Waters. It just took a lot longer for this one to catch on.

CHAPTER 3

It's Wine

*I have trodden the winepress alone, and I know
that it is hard to be really useful.*

—T. S. ELIOT

Once the grapes were dumped into the plastic bin, I changed into disposable clothes, ones that were destined for grape stains. I washed off my legs, got on a ladder, and, much to the amusement of the Pellegrini staff, hopped in. As far as temperature was concerned, jumping into the vat was not much different from plunging into Maine coastal waters. My toes went bloodless. Trying to ward off frostbite, I experimented with stomping techniques, including pacing, circling, zigzagging, all the movements aimed at breaking enough berries to create just enough juice so that the yeast could start to ferment. The fruit flies started to buzz, and after twenty minutes, I hosed myself down and saw an unexpected benefit from the project. My feet and legs were exfoliated smooth; no wonder there's an explosion of vine health-care products.

Nurselike, Dan the cellar master came by to take the grape's vital statistics: acidity, pH, and the concentration of sugar (Brix). The higher the Brix, the higher the finished alcohol. We wanted to hit a final alcohol of 14 percent, but as the grapes came in at 26 Brix we were headed for something more elevated, Kevin said.

"What will we do?" I asked.

He folded his arms against his short-sleeved, plaid shirt. "We'll figure it out," he said in a tone that was imbued with "trust me." I admit, it had the opposite effect. "You going to change out of your clothes, or are you going to go back to town sticky?" he asked.

I headed off to get out of my shorts, but along the way, I saw Dan. From the way he was walking, I knew he was on remote control. He carried a can with a hose and was walking toward my bin. Sulfur! I knew it! Damn it, I was going to have to watch them left and right in this place. I sped over to my tank and threw my body like a human shield in front of it. "Dan!" I shouted. "No!"

The young man looked over to Kevin as if to say, Where did you pick up this chick?

"Is that sulfur?" I urgently asked, thinking this little experiment of mine could be over in a flash. We were trying to hold off on adding sulfur until all the fermentations were finished, because I firmly believed that sulfur could kill off some of the yeasts that could be beneficial in the long run. My preference was to add only a little sulfur at bottling, but if we could get through malolactic fermentation, when the harsh malic acid goes through a natural and softening transformation, I'd be happy. I was so inexperienced at this: I thought that sulfur was blasted instead of dissolved into the crushed grapes.

"No," he said, "it's carbon dioxide. Keeps the fruit flies off."

I was relieved, but embarrassed because I was so inexperienced I didn't even know how sulfur was applied. The fruit flies were problematic and could increase the potential for a volatile acidity that could destroy the wine. Kevin and Dan convinced me that the carbon dioxide, in frozen form as a blast of dry ice, would be essential after every *pigeage* (foot stomping) until the wine started to ferment. Then it would create its own protective carbon dioxide. Yet, I later found out and saw for myself that covering the vat with a lid or even with a cloth or a clean sheet would have sufficed.

"But, I'm confused," Dan said. "What's the problem with sulfur?"

Dan believed in sulfur as almost everyone who studies wine formally does.

"We're doing native yeast fermentation on the wine, so we're not adding anything at all, even the goddess sulfur dioxide," I explained. "The sulfur would kill the yeast or at least most of it off. And," I continued, lips turning blue, "a wine is just more lively with less sulfur."

Looking to Kevin for support, I saw he was behind me nodding his head in affirmation. "And no feeding the yeast with diammonium phosphate (DAP), either," I said. "Or anything. No nitrogen."

"Really?" Dan asked.

"No diammonium phosphate, magnesium sulfate, yeast hulls, thiamine, folic acid, niacin, or calcium pantothenate."

Dan was game enough, a nice guy, but this was outside of his comfort zone. He was raised the way that most of us were—technology was good—and what I had to say just seemed crazy to him. I knew I would have to be hypervigilant in my role as wine cop. I had to keep a careful eye on that wine, to make sure nothing was going to slip in behind my back. Winemaking is excessively boring and appealing only to those with patience. I knew that most people working in wineries feel compelled to be active in a very passive process. This reflex *to do something*, anything, is worse in the New World, where there is more of a disconnect between working the vineyards and making the wine. By the time the grapes come in, the winemaker is antsy to feed the impulse to exercise that hand of man.

After my tirade, Dan blasted the top of the bin with the dry ice. The bin disappeared under a white cloud, and the fruit flies vanished. Then he put the bin on a forklift and moved it to the slightly colder room where Pellegrini keeps its wine in barrels. It felt as if he was wheeling an infant away from the mother into the nursery. Saddened, I finally changed into civilian clothes.

Kevin might have been right when he said the most important activity in winemaking was cleaning, but clearly the most exciting activity in making wine is *pigeage*—feeling the start, beginning, and end of the fermentation with your body. I had this opportunity one or two times a day when I got into the crate of grapes. Each day, there was more volume. At first, my feet sank in just a bit to cover the top of the foot, and three days into the practice, I was past my ankle. Every day, there was more and more juice from my foot stomping; by day four, it was up to my knees, but no sign of fermentation. By Sunday, I was drastically underemployed, weary of waiting for my "pot of water" to boil. Luckily, I received an e-mail from a nearby friendly winemaker I had been keeping my eyes on. Kevin Kelley, who makes wines for Lioco, his own Pinot and Chardonnay Salinia, as well as an exciting project he was to tell me about, asked me to come over and stomp for him. I asked permission from my chief winemaker. Kevin encouraged me to go. "You should see what it's like when it's the de facto method," he said.

Feeling unfaithful, I took off for Santa Rosa and drove into the most unlikely winery; it was located in a professional strip mall park. There among the office buildings was the headquarters for the Salinia winery. Kevin Kelley was about to make the first vintage of what was to become the widely popular Natural Process Alliance (NPA), a no-sulfur wine bottled in reusable stainless containers and intended for drinkers within one hundred miles of the winery.

Even while Kevin Kelley went to University of California–Davis, he knew he wanted to make wine with little or no sulfur and with nothing added or taken away, something that would give the professors there intense agita. He was totally up for naked wine. In spite of his surfer looks and California-born-and-bred demeanor, he had picked up a few tricks other than *pigeage* when he apprenticed in Burgundy. But his graciousness in giving a guest food or drink immediately was something he could have learned in Italy. First we had an espresso. We followed this with his homemade fig grappa—delicious. I asked him why he liked to use the stomp method instead of modern techniques. He told me it gives him the opportunity to understand the grapes with all his senses. "The texture of the grapes and stems tells you the ripeness level," he said. "The temperature gradient shows you where the variety of yeasts, including the essential *Saccharomyces cerevisiae*, are congregating. The gentle crackling sound of a young fermentation talks of yeast populations, and the aromatic mixture of fresh tree fruit and berries, earthy bread dough from the *Saccharomyces*, and vinyl from *Kloeckera* reveals the explosive microscopic world."

Dressed in my treading outfit, I sprayed myself with distilled grape alcohol, which Kevin said is the best disinfectant. I climbed up the ladder to a tank that was much deeper than I was used to. I could have swum in it had it been filled with liquid. Instead, it was stuffed with whole bunches of Syrah. A blast of ethyl acetate blew into my nostrils. I was alarmed. Every year, some poor worker dies while doing this seemingly harmless stunt. In fact, just two nights before, I read about two who died in a vat in Bordeaux. Death by carbon dioxide comes quickly.

"Hey, Kevin," I called out. "Did you read about those two guys who died in Bordeaux while treading grapes?"

"Don't worry, there's not enough carbon dioxide in there to get you yet."

"Tell me about the smell," I asked, worried that the smell of volatility could be a sign that bad bugs were spelling disaster in the nubile wine. Kevin was not worried in the least.

"That's your first clue—polish remover (the ethyl acetate)— that fermentation is about to start," he said.

Unlike the individual grapes I had been working on back at Pellegrini, here the whole clusters were attached to their stems. This made for a very uneven, scratchy, and dense surface, and it was much more difficult than my Sagrantino. I had to exert great effort to break the berries, so I jigged on top of them. By the time I had finished, there was only about an inch of juice on top of the fruit. It was like a mat of fruit with a slight slick of clay.

It was such a heavy and depressing day. I was a little sticky from grapes and humidity when I left Kevin Kelley, and I was missing the New York City edge when I hung a right in front of the Pellegrini Winery, just next to the old Carignan vines. I pulled onto the crush pad and let myself into the barrack-like winery. The industrial lights were dimmed, and my footsteps echoed off the walls. Dan had gone home, and Kevin was quiet. He's not much of a talker, anyway, but I could tell something was up.

"I'm going to hop in, and then we can go back, OK?" I asked.

"I already took care of the vat."

"You did what?"

"I punched it down. You weren't around, so I took care of it."

We were fighting over our child. I was the neglectful parent; he had already picked the kid up from school. I had become very attached to my one task, treading. I went to look at the child, the plastic bin in the middle aisle of the ten-ton stainless steel tanks. I looked at the vitals, the daily temperature and reading of how dry the wine might be getting. There was very little movement. I was grateful it hadn't taken its first steps while I was off gallivanting. With nothing more to be done but to get back and think about dinner, we left. In the car, Kevin started off the conversation, both of us feeling nauseous.

"I know you originally were going to make wine at Eyrie Vineyards and create your own wine," he said. "Here, it's a group effort—and I feel that you're a little disconnected."

We drove back to Healdsburg barely speaking until we reached his bungalow, which was still hidden behind unpruned overgrowth. There we sat, the car filling up with our breath and fogging the windows.

From how red in the face he was getting, I could tell that this was not going to be pleasant. "I don't understand," he started. This was getting very personal. Right or wrong, I felt as if Mr. Hamel and I had been involved and he was accusing me of sleeping with another man, when all I did was run off and stomp on someone else's grapes.

"I've been trying to make this work for you, but you have completely disengaged," he said. He hit the steering wheel, and I flinched.

Kevin was right. I knew I had disengaged, from the beginning, when I was prevented from grape picking. It was just as I had been told by champagne producer Stanislas Henriot. When you sever the farmer's tie with the land, you sever the emotional tie with the wine. I had felt that in my own way.

"So we're not Oregon!" he yelled.

"Of course not."

"You just hate California!"

This was so complicated. But he was wrong. I'd grown fond of the state, even if it did feel somewhat foreign, more foreign than the hills of Piemonte or the Loire, where I feel more at home. I have a New Yorker's view of the country, I'm afraid. I spend much time trying to figure out the differences between east and west, the way we taste, the way we feel. The Old World made more sense to me; it was connected, direct, and smaller. It was less politically correct and seemed to have more irony, and I just felt more comfortable around ancient architecture. The wineries and winemakers I dealt with made wines from the earth as an expression, not toward a perceived market taste. Even their sense of humor made more sense to me. Often, there could be argument, even yelling, but everyone was closer for it. And without a doubt, the taste of wine, leaner and more acidic, was more to my liking.

Even though Kevin and I were just friends, we would always have this love child, the Sagrantino. I was thinking about that love child when he asked me, "What do you want to do about the alcohol?"

"What do you mean, 'do'?" I asked, just as I had asked about the punch-down. I was back into the argument. Pain! And this felt like a further assault. "Aren't you the one who said, 'We'll let the wine make itself'?" Inwardly, I was thinking, *Right, what a cliché.*

"We have a serious problem, Alice," he said. "We talked about this last week. The alcohol is probably going to be about fifteen or sixteen. It's too high." Water addition, Kevin informed me, was the best option—economical and the gentlest solution.

This was heartbreak. "You're just punishing me!" I said, not believing that he wasn't using this water thing as a symbol.

"You're being a baby!" he said.

He justly chastised me. I was emotionalizing a situation that should have been objective, not subjective. I was pouting, sulking because there I was, making someone else's wine instead of my own. I was experiencing firsthand the dilemma of the New World winemaker who is land poor. Water. I had never considered it as even in the picture.

My stomach churned as it digested the question that would lead me to harsh reality. All I had to do was accept the word *do*. But did we have to *do* anything to the Sagrantino wine?

Obviously, yes.

Fifteen years ago, the wine industry picked its grapes when they reached 21, 22, or 23 degrees Brix, and the alcohol in wine ranged from 11.5 to 13 percent. Today, the Brix is often higher (following fashion and, some claim, climate change). And that corresponds to a higher alcohol level.

To estimate what kind of alcohol grapes are capable of producing, a conversion rate of 60 percent is applied to the degree of Brix. An increasingly hot topic is how so many modern wines are completely out of balance, because of ultrahigh alcohol levels, resulting from grapes that approach 30 degrees Brix. These high-alcohol wines are sometimes closer to fortified wine (Port, Sherry, etc.) than to table wine. Our Sagrantino had a Brix of 26. According to the math, without intervention, the final alcohol level on our wine could be 15.5 percent. Our acidity measured 0.56 percent (Kevin says that somewhere between 0.6 and 0.7 percent is optimal), and the pH was 3.87. The acidity was a little too low, the pH was a little too high. I was depressed, but we were still lucky. Sagrantino tends to hold on to its acidity longer than many other grapes. The wine was going to have reasonable natural acidity, which would add freshness. But the high sugars not only could create high alcohol, but could also put us in danger of something called a stuck fermentation—a situation that occurs when, as those in the Beaujolais found out, lactobacillus problems result in the *piqûre lactique* or when the yeast, gobbling the sugar, peters out before the wine ferments to dry. Correcting that problem might lead to heavy-duty intervention—which I wasn't happy about—in what I was hoping would be a natural wine.

The high-tech response for the alcohol problem is removing some of the alcohol. For taste as well as philosophical reasons, I am against extreme tools, like reverse osmosis or spinning cone to reduce the alcohol level. My low-tech response is to use a larger canopy on the vine, just as they did in the old days, to shade the grapes and make the fruit ripen more slowly, and to pick earlier. But these were no longer options for us.

"Most people do it," Kevin said, as our fight neutralized. Few talk about it outside the shop. As a colleague put it, "We just pick the fruit when it tastes really good—then we water it back in the winery." Kevin laughed, trying to chide me out of my mood and trying to win me over to water. He rationalized that adding water was merely replacing moisture sucked out of the grapes by the hot, dry fall winds.

Paul Draper, the founder of Ridge Winery and one of the most respected U.S. winemakers, talked about watering:

> We have, on occasion, added small amounts of water to a fermenter of zinfandel when a heat spike has pushed up sugars in a parcel before we were able to harvest it given the

number of other parcels that have ripened at the same moment. It is a problem that zinfandel can over ripen virtually overnight when temperatures rise precipitously. Water additions to rehydrate the grapes that have had water pulled out of them by the plant under heat stress must be done with the same light touch that is required for correct chaptalization in Europe. Careful water additions, like careful chaptalization, do not destroy the character of place in the wine, which can (otherwise) be destroyed by reverse osmosis and other mechanical processes.

Draper and Kevin aside, I could hear my diehard *vin naturel* friends in France condemning me for "not listening to what the grapes want to do." It was too late for that; the grapes wanted to be picked earlier. "Next year," Kevin said. That night, before retiring, I wrote to Filippo Antonelli in Montefalco. I suppose I was looking more for permission than advice.

The next morning, Kevin was making the coffee and slicing tomatoes. I sat at his kitchen table, looking over my e-mail. "Filippo!" I said. "He says yes to the water."

I read aloud the e-mail: "'In Italy we go to jail if we add water. So I never do it. If in California you're allowed? Do it!'"

But I didn't ask Kevin when we were going to add the water, and I guess I was still hoping he'd forget.

In the morning, the temperature of the juice still hadn't much budged. I would have been a neurotic mother—worry, worry, worry. So it was no surprise that I fretted about the vat. The fermentation, however, had started with a very subtle, almost imperceptible prickle that I felt on my legs. My hopes were raised, yet the next day, fizz or no fizz, the grapes and the juice still made my toes go numb with cold. We had gone five days so far and had seen just the hint of some smoke, but clearly no fire. I worried that the winery was too cool for the fermentation to get serious. I had to head back to New York soon, and I longed to see the grapes start to ferment. Remembering how bread loves a warmish spot to rise, I suggested to my winemaker that we place the bin outside in the last of the Indian summer days.

Kevin was amused. Because of my passion for natural wine, he couldn't resist joking with me. "Isn't that temperature control?" he asked. "Manipulation?"

Yes and no. There is a range of about 30 degrees for safe fermentation. Too high, perhaps over 90 degrees, and, as I do in the heat, the yeast poops out. Too low, under 60 degrees, and the yeast falls into suspended animation. Anyway, isn't fermenting in the weather, in the outdoors, a true representation of the vintage, I rationalized?

Lower and slower temperatures achieve enhanced aromatics; higher and faster temperatures often extract more tannin and develop a more masculine wine. These days, using heating and cooling coils inside a tank, or jackets on the outside, is considered necessary for modern winemaking.

"It gives me some assurance that temperature won't get out of control overnight—which can happen in larger fermenters, five tons and up," Kevin said. "On the other hand, while I was winemaker at Preston, I had a tank of Cinsault which I planned to ferment cool (no higher than seventy-eight degrees), and at one point, it took off and got into the low nineties. After fixing the glitch, we then controlled the degrees as planned. The wine had a juiciness to it that I not seen before. I ascribed it to that short heat spike, and I did the fermentation that way in subsequent vintages."

Old-fashioned temperature control used to be literally opening and closing doors and windows. But, of course, the weather was never the same. The season leaves an imprint on the wine just as native yeasts do. And I like that. I was happy to find that I was not alone, even among those who use large fermenters. Heinrich Breuer, a winemaker in the Rheingau in Germany, ferments in a warmish cellar in large, oval, wooden vats. "Temperature control for wine is like never letting your children feel fresh air," he said. "I would never use control."

"Don't give me a hard time! Just help me!" I said to my wine-maker. "This is way more natural than being cooped up from the weather inside stainless steel!"

Solicitously, Kevin drove our bin of Sagrantino outside to the crush pad. Its temperature was 65.9 degrees. The Brix was starting its decline; it was now down to 23.9 from its earlier 26-plus, which told us that something was going on. I hopped in and worked the grapes over gently with my feet, sinking in up to right below my knees. There were some warm spots in corners, but mostly, even though the rays were strong on my back, my feet were still chilled.

Two days after the wine's day in the sun, we had a tumultuous and lusty ferment—true purple prose. Vitals statistics were 16 degrees Brix, 76.2 degrees Fahrenheit. A spongy collection of grape skins and pulp had pushed to the top. Underneath by a good fourteen inches lurked the foamy, vibrant, magenta, fermenting juice. Those yeasts were stuffing themselves silly on the sugar, like a teenage boy on Thanksgiving turkey.

Ten days after I started the process of turning Sagrantino grapes into wine and using my feet to hasten things along, it was time to take care of my life back on the East Coast. The wine was in midfermentation, and it wasn't clear how long it would take to complete the alcoholic fermentation. To my knowledge, we had added nothing to it—no yeast, no yeast nutrients, no sulfur, no enzymes.

As I was getting ready to leave California, I had separation anxiety. Before I headed to the airport, I stopped by the winery for a last look.

The bin of one and a half tons of fermenting juice sat alone among the Pellegrini Family Vineyards' stainless steel fermenting vats. I fetched a glass and dipped it in to taste the wine. It was still so tannic I laughed in surprise; it was definitely less sweet and had developed a Middle Eastern cinnamon spiciness. The thermometer read 79 degrees, and the Brix had gone down all the way to 13.0. But we still had to get it down to minus 1.3 for it to be dry, and that is where it would be when I returned.

I was dressed for the flight and was not eager to spend the five hours in the air sticking to my seat. So instead of my farewell plunge, I opted for the conventional punch-down, submerging the cap, as Kevin would do in my absence, with a long stainless steel rod. The day before, the cap looked like a bunch of plump, shiny Alphonso olives; now it looked more like drying pomace. It was starting to run to home. When I tried to shove the rod under, the cap resisted me; it was so stubborn, I couldn't budge it. So, I rolled my pants to my thigh and climbed over. I wasn't going to jump in—the juice had become so deep that I'd have drenched my pants—and my jeans wouldn't have added anything special to the wine process, or the flavor. As I supported myself on the edge of the bin, my toes effortlessly pierced the cap. The shocking whoosh of foaming life rose to the top. No less than thrilling. It was just fermenting like crazy. Such energy, such life. This was the cool part. No tool could ever work this effectively. Beneath the grape solids, the wine was finally and delightfully warm. It was a parting gesture, because I would be back in two weeks to be there for the pressing off.

But that's getting ahead of the story. On this day, twenty days after the grapes were picked, the wine's activity was slowing down. There was still a gentle snap and pop from the carbon dioxide being released by yeasts consuming sugar.

Kevin said, "Even though the Brix and alcohol numbers barely move at this point, and you could doubt that there's life left in the process, you can see that fermentation is ongoing because the cap is still buoyant."

It was true; the cap of grape skins, pulp, and seeds floating on top of the wine was still springy.

"At the point that the cap falls into the wine," Kevin said, "we'll know that the yeasts have petered out and that fermentation has taken its final bow."

After two weeks away, getting twice-daily updates, I returned for pressing off the juice. When I saw my child, the cap was still thick, but it barely offered any resistance when it was pushed back into the drink. Where, before, the wine was furiously fermenting and there had been a purple-haze whoosh when I jabbed it down. In its place now was gentle and quickly vanishing foam.

But tasting the wine and feeling its evolution were the best of all. I couldn't perceive any sweetness, though there was still plenty of cherry confit laced with cinnamon, cardamom, and white pepper. The texture was gorgeous and firm, like wide-wale corduroy, and the tannins were heavy on the tongue.

I chuckled. "That's different," I said. "That's thrilling! It's wine!"

The first big chapter for my Sagrantino grapes, the most dramatic, was coming to a close. The wine, born on October 24, 2008, would have had thirty-two days of fermentation and maceration and was safely swishing between a womb of grape garbage left on the bottom and a thick layer of seeds and skins on the top. One of the last tasks was to separate it swiftly and safely from this protective sac.

For this we needed two tools—a transfer pump and a stainless steel bin equipped with a mesh sieve. We pushed one end of the pump's hose into our bin of grapes. I pointed the other end at the mesh sieve. The crud collected on top and the pure wine collected in the bin.

That clear wine, called free-run juice, came from my foot stomping, or *pigeage*, of the grapes, the manual punch-down, and natural grape pressure. But there was another part of the process. We needed to press off the wine still trapped in the leftover grape solids. The result would be called the press wine.

When the pump could pump no more (it was down to mostly sludge), it was time for physical labor. We found a pair of size 6 Wellies, left over from a small-footed winemaker who had been an intern in 2007. I washed them off and hopped over the bin, shovel in hand. I started to dig away at the huge mound of solid grape bits, pitching them with great effort over the bin wall onto the sieve. This was much more strenuous than shoveling wet snow, especially if you're like me, a former dancer, middle-aged wimp with a body that defies producing upper body strength. I couldn't finish the job, and Kevin took over. And yes, I felt like a humbled yet coddled journalist.

The solids were transferred to a press, from which Kevin and I took sips. The stuff was so bitter that we had our doubts. Press wine is often so good that it gets blended into the free run, but we weren't so sure that this wine would add anything positive. Time would tell. The first press would be raised in a separate barrel, an old oak barrel, and when it was finished, Kevin would decide what its fate would be.

After dinner that night, he and I layered on sweaters and polar fleece and went out for a walk. The fog hung heavy. Small lanterns of orange persimmons seemed to jump out of the mist. We walked around Healdsburg, looking for the plump, firm Fuyu persimmons to pluck. It was shivery cold when I asked, "Kevin, when do we add the water?" It was dark, so I couldn't see his face as he told me that when I wasn't looking, he had dropped in two buckets of five gallons of water each. It was so dark, he couldn't see my face. Even though I had known it was coming, I felt saddened and cheated. If it had to be done, I wanted to do the deed myself.

Another red-eye flight to New York City was in my future that night. I got on board knowing that the wine had been sent off to boarding school, one with headmaster Kevin in charge.

As with any kid, this young wine faced a future with many possible pitfalls. It could fall in with the wrong crowd (bad bacteria). It could be fiercely independent (taking forever to be ready). What I knew for sure was that the Sagrantino would be a totally different wine after its puberty—the second fermentation, malolactic fermentation, turns the harder and sharper malic acid into softer and rounder lactic acid. And any bottled wine will be totally different from the high-toned, tannic, and cinnamon one I spirited away in two vials and smuggled onto the plane to savor on my flight back.

CHAPTER 4

A Wine's Song

The habit of regarding "art" as a thing apart from life is fatal to the development of taste.
—EDITH WHARTON

T hat's a big one," I whispered to my young friend Pascaline. She was shoulder to shoulder with me down in Nicolas Joly's cramped vat room. We had just descended the steep stairs beneath the kitchen of La Coulée de Serrant in the Cotswold-esque Loire village of Savennières. We were stunned to see, among the darkened barrels holding the year's vintage of Chenin Blanc, a tuning fork big enough to musically align a rhinoceros.

Joly has become the Deepak Chopra of wine biodynamics. Bio-dynamics, a form of agriculture developed by twentieth-century philosopher Rudolf Steiner, promotes healthy soil and views agri-culture holistically. Its practitioners believe in the ability of bio-dynamics to heal the earth from past harms. The tools are treatments using a core of nine preparations derived from plant, mineral, and animal material and can range from stinging nettles to silica to cow dung. Joly's promotion of Steiner's approach to farming, with its link to the moon's phases, has been tireless: writing books, creating a fabulous roving wine tasting, and ceaselessly educating. Seeing us in awe of the U-shaped object, he offered his explanation: "I've been thinking about what makes a wine. I am very interested in this sort of thing, the song. A wine must have a song."

Before Joly reclaimed his family's domaine in the 1980s, he was a banker. The man has the air of the aristocrat philosophy student; he was always thinking. His statement almost gave us belly laughs, because he said it with such solemnity. It was near cliché, but true enough. Music triggers emotional responses, and this is what he was looking for in a wine—that vibration of life, the connection to emotions.

You can look for a caretaker with a list of skills and qualities; you can write a personal ad for a wine as well: "Wanted: a wine that has a strong, jamlike quality; has no scratch; and is very smooth. Tastes good on walks on the beach at sunsets." But to say, "Wanted: a wine that has the rhythm of truth in it," is not quantifiable. To put it in his words, a song. Not a commercially canned arrangement, but a creation that resonates and vibrates.

Joly was obsessive, but in the best way. I could see that there were more songs in store for us.

Just after Pascaline and I left (we were to return after lunch for a special tasting), she took me to see her friend, the winemaker Benoit Courault and his Anjou vines. We arrived at what looked like a shack and climbed out of the car. Outside the structure, a bunch of merry men, vignerons, and friends were waiting for us

around an old, upright barrel, drinking hard cider. After the hellos
and introductions (and our morning cider), we were off to see
Ben's vineyards. The day was cold and the ground was crunchy
underfoot. The vines seemed glassed under ice, and in short time,
so were my feet. The visit was thankfully short, and we returned
to the shack/vat room where ringlet-haired Ben gathered his
pipette and tasting glasses and put on some music. Tom Waits
filled the air—"Waltzing Matilda." I couldn't blame it on jet lag.
The song unlocked a moment of love lost. To my embarrassment,
Pascaline's shock, and the amusement of the others, I burst into
tears and pleaded for different music.

A wine can have the same effect on me that Waits does. The reaction goes beyond science. A technical wine cannot provoke me
in this way. There's an emotional truth in natural wine that I can't
ignore.

Let me rewind to the day before the music began. It was the last
week of January 2009, and going to the Loire at this time of year
had become my habit since 2000. Others gear up for Paris's Fashion Week, but on my calendar, these early winter days belong to
dégustation. Dragging my wheeled bag behind me, I sprinted the
short distance from the Angers TGV to Pascaline's apartment.
She and I had become family almost from the moment I met her
in Paris, one of those instant connections that result from similarities of mind and palate.

"Coucou!" she shouted into the intercom and scampered down
the stairs, and with puppy energy, threw her arms around me. The
talented girl is so narrow and so strong from the heavy lifting that
comes from being a sommelier. Her small button of a chin tempers
that broad, innocent moon face while angular glasses unfairly com-
municate a "Don't mess with me" persona.

Once settled in, she popped the cork on something fizzy. This is a tradition that more Americans should have. Walk in, get bubbles. Perfect. Civilized.

Workaholics, we sat in parallel play on our respective computers in her warm kitchen. I sipped and absentmindedly asked about our plans: "Benoit and Patrick's tomorrow, and then?"

Then a Facebook message arrived, and it changed our calendar.

"'My father wants me to ask you to join us for the annual tasting,'" I read aloud. "'As we have a few Americans, to have a US opinion would be interesting.'"

Listening intently, Pascaline guessed, "That's from Virginie?"

Virginie Joly was Nicolas's daughter. One of the most anticipated tastings on our schedule was their Return to Terroir, otherwise known as La Renaissance des Appellations. This pop-up tasting has been a powerful ambassadorship for biodynamics and is arguably the best showcase for biodynamic wines. Joly started this road show—he takes winemakers around the globe—in 2000, when he had three fistfuls of wineries to show off. Now he has in his organization close to two hundred domaines practicing or starting to practice Steiner's form of biodynamic agriculture.

Biodynamics is an agricultural pursuit with a philosophic point of view. But because it sounds mystical, the practice can invite controversy, fear, and derision. Granted, this approach to farming with its ritual and rhythm can seem a little woo-woo to anyone who insists on science. New converts seem to love publicity shots with them packing cows horns filled with dung and burying them in the ground, where the objects will ferment and transform into a sweet-smelling fertilizer. The fertilizer is great and the media shot a bit cliché and a little annoying, but nevertheless, the proof is in the stellar vignerons Joly had assembled as members of his group. And what's more, if it is not healing the earth, this kind of farming is exceedingly kind to it.

But, Demeter USA, the stateside certifier of biodynamic farms, is steps ahead of Europe's certifying arm. Not only does Demeter USA establish farming rules, but it sets winemaking parameters as well. I asked the Demeter president, Jim Fullmer, a biodynamic strawberry farmer in Oregon, why give a certification to a wine— or to the process of winemaking. He answered that of course, the practice refers to farming, but it is in the spirit of biodynamics to safeguard the processing also, so that the vitality from the farming isn't lost. "You know better than I," he wrote, "all the things one can do to a wine. Imagine biodynamic yogurt preserved with potassium sorbate and colored with red dye #40? No thanks."

In this context, he said that wine shouldn't be judged separately from the process that produced it. Demeter USA molded the biodynamic wine standard to the idea that the food has to be as true to the agriculture it came from as possible.

After years of back-and-forths, the organization created standards for two categories—wine made from biodynamic grapes and biodynamic wine. Both standards forbid external yeasts, enzymes, or pasteurization. Both categories have limits on sulfur, but that amount has wiggle room.

Joly's Renaissance group doesn't award certification, but it awards stars to the wines they accept into their traveling show, handing out one to three. These are meant to be encouraging for those who are just starting out. The group's basic requirement is farming; no synthetic chemical is allowed in the vineyard. Nor is there an allowance for genetically modified or aromatic yeasts.

With each star, the wines get closer to natural winemaking, all
with the goal of celebrating terroir. Oddly, though, sulfur is not
addressed, while biodynamic certifications limit its addition.

Right now, biodynamic certification is the best means by which
the public can determine how unprocessed a wine is. It is not perfect; it does not adequately address the usage of sulfur. But it is
still a decent bet for recognizing this category of wine. Nevertheless, Fullmer cautioned against putting too much emphasis on the
Demeter certification as a definition of "natural":

> In my humble opinion the Demeter® Wine Standard is not
> THE "natural" wine standard, yet I guess one could say it
> is one "natural" wine standard. That, however, was not nec-
> essarily the goal. The way the Demeter® wine standard
> evolved was not as a quest to define "natural" wine. It was
> the Demeter® Processing Standard, applicable to *many*
> product types as it is applied to wine. The theme of the
> Demeter® Processing Standard, whether it be cheese,
> bread, baby food, olive oil or wine, is simply to not manip-
> ulate the biodynamic agricultural ingredients used so that
> they define the product. Are biodynamic "natural" prod-
> ucts? I personally think so—but that word "natural" has lit-
> erally been beaten to death. Our primary concern is about
> maintaining the integrity of biodynamic agriculture, not
> really trying to define "natural."

What gets the Renaissance, as well as the other alternative tasting groups, in a snit is the seeming stupidity of the French Appellation system and the European Union. The bureaucracies there
are working overtime to make terroir irrelevant while pushing EU

winemakers into more commercial winemaking so that the wine-makers will be "competitive." Often, the purest examples of place are not awarded appellations status, because they don't taste "right." For example, Thierry Puzelat, the fine producer from the Loire, explained with resignation that some of the grapes he works with and that made his reputation—his Pineau d'Aunis and Menu Pineau and Chenin—will be sold only as Vin de Table by 2016:

> After 2016, the only whites allowed where I work will be Sauvignon, and, for the reds, Gamay, Cabernet Franc, and Côt. Our own special varieties, which made our region unique, will be forbidden. In fact, the Touraine authorities want to make all of the Sauvignon Blanc into something like people expect Sancerre to taste like, so it's easier for the consumer to understand. They employed New Zealand oenologist Sam Harrop to explain to the winemakers what they should produce for the international market—only the aromatic Sauvignon.

Puzelat's Sauvignon has nothing in common with New Zealand gooseberry or what is known as the "grassiness" or "cat pee" of a Sancerre. It is unique to itself, leaning toward green freshness and melon. The wine is complex and reflects both the man and his ground. In defiance, Puzelat added that he was grafting over some of his Sauvignon to replant the soon-to-be-outlawed Menu Pineau: "I will soon organize my life as a table wine producer."

Because of the laws, he won't be able to put Appellation d'origine contrôlée (AOC) Touraine on the label if his white wine isn't Sauvignon. His only option is to label it Vin de Table (VdT), which also means he will not be allowed to give his wine a vintage on the label. And for this reason, it is getting sexy to see VdT on a bottle. Among a certain crowd, who work naturally, it's almost a badge of courage. It says, to hell with the authorities who are policing the market—we want authenticity!

It doesn't matter at all what is on the label for Joly's group. As long as the board members of the group hear the song, the wine and winemaker are in the door. It's about that emotional response to wine. Terroir is an emotional response. It cannot be quantified.

The Renaissance tasting is filled with discoveries at every table; the winemaking is at a very high level. Known for high quality, the tasting is also something of a meal ticket for the winemakers who are part of the group. These shows are attended by distributors, journalists, and wine buyers. Having the Renaissance's stamp of approval is meaningful to a world increasingly looking for "authentic" and, ultimately, salable.

And so, with all this background in mind, I reread the Facebook invitation as I sat at Pascaline's kitchen table.

"What do you think?" I asked Pascaline, as if there was a question. Sure, we had plans, but the opportunity to meet this rarefied, privileged group of top-tier biodynamic winemakers at a tasting and to experience how they tasted wine from America seemed to me an unprecedented one. My vote would not count at the gathering; I would be there to illuminate, perhaps explain, flavors and techniques to the group.

So there I was, driving with Pascaline to Nicolas's the next day, after a delicious lunch of fresh-caught mackerel, yet I still felt fragile from my morning's emotional experience and frozen from a morning in Benoit's vineyards. Pascaline and I walked to the eleventh-century monastery building where the sacred meeting of biodynamic elders was taking place. We warmed our butts by the large wood-burning stove and waited for the board meeting to end and for them to take their seats at the long, narrow table laden with narrow INAO glasses (wine-tasting glasses approved by Institute National des Appellations d'Origine and invented with input from Chauvet). On another table, I eyeballed about a hundred bottles waiting for evaluation. The doors opened, and out walked the celebrities, the superstars of biodynamic wines. Most came from France, but also Joly's right-hand man, Stefano Bellotti, from Italy. We took our seats, and Pascaline, grinning a smile that shouted *high-five!* seized a chair right next to one of her wine goddesses, Burgundy's Anne-Claude Leflaive.

Tasting commenced. If I had ever thought I was judgmental about wine, I was a pussycat compared with this crowd. I have sometimes insulted friends because I've rejected their taste in champagne, for instance, or called something undrinkable because I couldn't get past the winemaking methods and resulting taste. But in this company, I had nothing to apologize for. None of us bothered being democratic about our sensibilities. We were all about Kant's "judgments of taste," meaning taste is both objective and subjective. They were looking for this song that resonated to a group of like-minded people.

Many of the wines were wrong for the group. All the wines from Germany were obviously yeasted and had so much sulfur I started to sneeze as though it were pollen season. An Australian Riesling provoked Stefano to proclaim that it was crap—no assessment—everything was judged on an emotional level. The tasters had their radar up for artificial flavor and texture, while Joly pronounced over and over his new phrase, often in English: "This wine had no song."

Finally, there was some hope. Stefano presented the San Fereolo Dolcetto. Before we tasted, he gave us one more piece of information. "There is only one problem: Her father is Italy's most important journalist," he joked.

There was no problem at all; the wine was the real thing. Dolcetto was dusty with a bright cherry, perhaps a little too concentrated but still not with terroir-canceling density. Daughter of a famous daddy or not, Nicoletta Bocca had charmed us with her wine.

Next up were the U.S. wines, and we soon tasted some more disasters. One Pinot Noir was coffee syrup. Another was marred by toasty new wood. Another was viciously acidified. Where before the wines were categorically dismissed, here the crowd demanded critical assessment. They wondered if perhaps they didn't know enough about American soil and terroir to make a judgment. All eyes were on me. I felt like saying, Hey, the wines are not my fault!

What still stumps my sensibilities is how people making technical, adjusted wines seek out to secure a place in this group with the stated goal of terroir, as achieved through the practice of biodynamics. Is the concept of expressing terroir so misunderstood? Were the winemakers so blinded by the commercial possibilities of inclusion into the group that they forgot that their products didn't meet certain very basic parameters?

"This is a phrase for you, Alice," Joly addressed me, tapping his middle fingers together for emphasis. "Mondo character. AOC Mondialization." He was absolutely perplexed with the disappointing market-driven quality of the American wines and seemed to take it personally.

I tried to break down why each rejected wine had failed. The resulting scene and exasperation seemed like a page from Edmund Burke's introduction to the *On Taste; On the Sublime and Beautiful; Reflections on the French Revolution:* "But should any man be found who declares, that to him tobacco has a taste like sugar, and that he cannot distinguish between milk and vinegar; or that tobacco and vinegar are sweet, milk bitter, and sugar sour; we immediately conclude that the organs of this man are out of order, and that his palate is utterly vitiated."

The offending winemakers thought they were displaying beautiful wines, but their products were more about style and less about place, in other words, "New World." The unfortunate tasters in this cold, monkish building were left stumped and confused. And so they reached to understand.

"Do they really all irrigate?" they asked. "Do they really add water to reduce the alcohol? Do they all yeast their wines? All of them?" Joly was not just disappointed; he was outraged. It was as if he took it personally that people submitted wines that so missed his point.

I assured him there were Americans working well, and I cited a few. And that is how I became a U.S. natural-winemaking apologist. What I hadn't counted on, however, was explaining the return-to-terroir point of view to California. Later, sitting in Pascaline's apartment and checking e-mail, I let out a dramatic *eek!*

She ran in the living room. "Are you okay?"

I read her the e-mail from a winery owner who was "pissed off . . . as my commitment to organic and biodynamic grape growing dates back thirty years and counting . . . and then to have people telling me that my wines do not represent terroir, without having ever seen my vineyard . . ."

Unbeknownst to me, Joly had informed this man, Robert Kamen, that Alice Feiring could explain everything. I remember meeting Kamen on two occasions in New York City, but I had forgotten about his wine's history, so I took the opportunity to visit his website. There I learned that his Sonoma property was certainly a pretty one. I often think that when many Americans talk of great terroir, they're actually saying they have a great view. Then, I read further. He talked about "luxury" winemaking. From the taste of his wine and the sound of his words, his total philosophy seemed in opposition to the group's and mine. I met him another time, when he came to a seminar at Crush, a wine store in New York City, where winemaker Eric Texier was holding forth on Syrah.

Kamen asked him, "So you're telling me that you actually don't use yeast for your wine?"

Texier replied that he'd never worked with it in his life.

Kamen and the Return-to-Terroir group had an important common value in farming, but that was it. Here it was again, that huge Old World/New World disconnect. Here was a winemaker who loves Burgundy and French wines. He visited these regions extensively. Yet he made ultraripe-fruit-driven, concentrated wines and bottled them up.

Joly called it song, I called it voice, but we meant the same thing. Just as writing needs a voice, a distinctive wine needs its own expression. The trouble is, how do you explain what a voice or a song or a tune is to a winemaker who is tone-deaf?

My visit to the Loire came to its end, and I was stateside before Lincoln's Birthday. By the time I arrived in New York City to my walk-up in Little Italy, there were three other e-mails waiting for me from other winemakers who did not make the cut. Joly's excuse for setting me up was that he knew I'd do a better job than he would. I began to see a pattern. I have gained a reputation that I'd do the dirty work of others. If a magazine wants a ten-most-overrated-wines list, the editors call me. If they want an editorial about the faults of the Californian wine industry, they call me. When someone wants to take on the commercial wine industry, he or she calls me.

I took on my responsibility and responded to all of the e-mails. But the only correspondent who wanted a dialogue was the man with the prettiest view.

I called Robert Kamen a few days later, after the jetlag had worn off. That initial call was brief because he needed to get off the phone quickly. "There is a man here digging a nine-hundred-foot well at eighty-five dollars a foot," he explained, "and there is some negotiation to attend to."

"Irrigation?"

"Oh, yeah," he said.

"Did you ever try to dry-farm?"

The question did not amuse him.

When he did call me back in an hour, I sucked in a breath and willed myself to be diplomatic and act as charged, as temporary ambassador. I told Kamen that his wine was too fruit driven, too concentrated, and too high in alcohol, and while the wine wasn't overly woody, the degree of fruit ripeness canceled out terroir.

He reiterated that was impossible, because his middle name was terroir.

"Let me put it to you this way," I said, trying to be polite but straight. "Your wine is good. There's no doubt about that. But the

Merlot and Cabernet taste as if the style of wine was chosen first and then you crafted it towards that goal."

"Exactly!" he said.

"This kind of winemaking is the opposite of the group's philosophy, where wine works with nature, the grape as an expression of the soil and not just the sun." And then I read him back the words on his site. "'Fully express the character of the vineyard while producing intense, highly extracted, terroir-driven wines.' To them, terroir isn't about high extraction," I said.

"That is a clear explanation," he said, much to my relief. He didn't thank me, though. Instead, he went on a tirade about how he had hand-delivered his wines to the Renaissance group. "I could have saved myself a lot of trouble if I had known what the group really was looking for—bacteria-ridden wines that were so natural, six bottles out of twelve had to be thrown out. I don't make that kind of wine. I have a business to run."

This bacteria-ridden, bottle-variation excuse was an oft-used one in recent rebukes of the natural-wine world. Without a doubt, sometimes—not always—the wines can be a little funky, a little reduced, a little edgy. But he was confusing biodynamic, which allows sulfur, with natural, which tries to do without. Even though many natural winemakers are biodynamic, not all biodynamic wines are "natural." But he was completely off mark with his stated need to run a business.

As Ridgely always said, "Sustainable means sustainable to the farmer." A winemaker must make a living. No argument there. A goal of consistency, however, is a very different mind-set.

André Simon, in his 1919 book *The Connoisseur's Textbook*, describes the difference between Old World and New World wines: "In the old world, winemaking is an art; in America, it is an industry." I'm not saying that industry doesn't happen in the Old World as well, but if we just add the term *mind-set* after *Old World*, then Simon's statement, almost one hundred years old, also applies to the modern era.

I hung up without sparring, taking the bait, or having the last word. If I had told the Sonoma winemaker about the people I had visited on the day Pascaline and I had stuffed our bellies full of mackerel, I'm sure he'd have been as disbelieving as he was when he questioned Eric Texier's use of natural yeast. I can't quite imagine what Kamen would have thought, for example, of Patrick Desplats's Les Griottes, and while this French winemaker is even more extreme than most, his work is far from an industry.

The first time I met Desplats, I thought his wines resembled the man: erratic and volatile, exactly the kind of wines that Kamen disparaged as bacteria-ridden. Desplats was new, rambunctious, and creative. Sometimes the wines worked; sometimes they didn't. These were a great example of those wines that could (and did) explode on the shelves; sometimes they were stable. They were, in fact, exactly the kinds of wines that gave no-sulfur winemaking a bad name.

Now, Desplats has grown up, well, at least a little. He still loves the party, but the newness and excitement has integrated into wine maturity. Pascaline and I had visited him the day we had attended Joly's tasting. Still searching, Desplats had given up biodynamics for a fascination with the farming philosophy of the Japanese master Masanobu Fukuoka, a sort of do-little kind of farming. His search for an agricultural foundation for his natural wines also led him to have some vines planted from seeds. As we tromped through the vines, he noted, "People today plant for thirty years. I plant for two hundred."

We headed back to the winery, a chicken coop that, with the windows broken, was as frozen inside as outside. Dostoyevsky's question about whether it is better to live in a chicken coop or a crystal palace came to mind. It was easy to contrast this manic, crazed energy, with all of his impetuousness and naïveté with the crystal palaces of expensive winemaking lands elsewhere. While I had been looking elsewhere, Desplats's wines had become terrific. This was February, and the red wines were still under the cap, six months after harvest. The nitrogen-rich yeast cells (the fine lees) seem to scavenge the oxygen from the wine and thus are used by winemakers looking to reduce or eliminate sulfur and make the wine more stable.

Pat Desplats wanted us to taste his Cabernet Franc, still on its skins, four months after the grapes had been picked. He tried to open the spigot but the juice refused to flow; it was frozen solid. After a little work, he was able to extract a trickle into the glass. As yet, there was no volatility, that little nail-polish-remover smell that can happen without sulfur and that scares off so many school-trained winemakers. There was, however, lots of velvet and touches of animal and blackberry. *Yes*, I wondered, *what would "Sonoma Robert" think of this man?* Many in the New World would not take this kind of winemaking seriously. They might discount it as not sustainable (financially) and not serious. Or they might think that I was merely charmed because it was quaint and rustic. Desplats is emblematic of those, biodynamic or not, who have a métier, not an industry, and are making fascinating wines that have a song. Like the music of Philip Glass or Shostakovich, his wine is not to everyone's taste. Was I asking too much of my home country, the United States, to make room for this kind of wine experience? Perhaps I was, I thought, feeling that I had asked too much of my own Sagrantino.

Months later, Pascaline arrived in New York City to take on wine director duties at Rouge Tomate. I installed her in the neighborhood, taking my own duties as her American mother seriously, ensuring that I could keep an eye on her. In June, the Sagrantino had not yet bottled, but Ridgely asked Kevin to seal up a half bottle for me, and he sent it along. When it arrived, I let it settle for a few days to get over being "air sick." Pascaline and I arranged a rendezvous to taste.

She arrived, garbed in T-shirt and cocky little hipster cap. I snapped up the bottle, stemware, and olives. I walked past the map of Burgundy tacked to the sickly green wall (my landlord's idea of a good joke) outside my door and climbed the rickety steps (which should be a Class 3 Housing Department violation) to my roof. Pascaline stepped into her professional role and played sommelier. She pulled out a tie from her pocket and knotted it around her neck. Then with a firm pop, she removed the cork. She poured. The color was a dark, dark blue-garnet. As if on cue, we simultaneously plunged our noses into the Riedel glass bowls. I swirled and smelled, and smelled it again as if I couldn't believe it. Actually, I couldn't believe it. The Sagrantino was very pretty. It made me laugh; it made me smile. "It's gorgeous," Pascaline gushed. "I'm very proud of you. I'd never have the nerve to do this."

Water addition be damned, I almost started to cry, and there was no Tom Waits playing.

CHAPTER 5

The Saints

There is a devil in every berry of the grape.
—KORAN

Overlooking the almost too-perfect rolling hills in the southern Beaujolais town of Charnay, at the end of a cul-de-sac, rests the home of the Texiers. I've known Eric Texier, a lapsed nuclear engineer turned winemaker, for not quite a decade. His vineyards are on the border between the northern and southern Rhône. He commutes an hour to his vines.

Eric and I first clicked over a famed Japanese farmer. We had both read the poetic memoir *One Straw Revolution*, which recounts how a onetime scientist came to a Zen-like interpretation of farming. People refer to the Japanese farmer's method as "natural" or "do-nothing" farming, but it is essentially "do-little." Eric even started a communal vineyard named after the man, Masanobu Fukuoka. This Fukuoka vineyard is just across from his winery, right on the outskirts of town. Then once we latched on to an ongoing debate about Chauvet, we were never at a loss for conversation.

Eric studied Chauvet as intently as my grandfather studied Talmud. Because the scientific writings would be way too difficult even in my own language, I relied on Eric's interpretations. To get into the belly of the beast, to talk to the winemakers who were there at the beginning of the Chauvet effect, I knew my friend would be a fearless sidekick for me. Luckily, he was agreeable. As we headed out in his truck to Villié-Morgon, I thanked him. He replied, "You're not exactly twisting my arm. After all, Marcel Lapierre and then dinner with Jean Foillard? Not a problem!"

A good-looking man with an easy smile and stylish rectangles of glasses, Eric often had a cigarette in his fingers and always wore his shirttails out. He had exchanged the lab-coat appearance for that of a hardworking vigneron—sturdy, huggable—and he always punctuated his thoughts with an ironic chuckle. I already knew that Eric had an analytic mind, was a searcher. He had initially started in a rather bold and modern winemaking style, but since then, he pulled back, finding his voice. I didn't know how he swapped his life out from nuclear scientist to working the vines. With a forty-five-minute drive ahead, I finally had the time to find out more of Eric's personal story.

"Nuclear scientist. How?" I asked. "I suppose transitioning from nuclear to vin naturel is not so strange. After all, Einstein decided at the end of his life he believed in God. You just got to it a little quicker."

"Ah, okay, I tell you," he said, as we drove past the experimental vineyard and I strained to see the little vines underneath their blanket of weeds and flowers. "It was very hypocritical to what I was doing. Nuclear is such a huge business for France. The truth is really not welcome, especially in the field I was working in:

earthquake resistance in nuclear disasters. It was really like—okay, is there a risk? Yes? How big is the risk? Huge? Not huge? Less than one hundred people? Ah, so there's no risk.

"At one point, I didn't want to play anymore. It's the same for those zero-sulfur guys, but who really do add sulfur. Even if you add a tiny bit, and you call yourself a hard-core no-sulfur guy, it isn't true. You can't lie. I hate when people lie, whether it is in science or in vin naturel."

Eric and I had more in common than our interest in Fukuoka and Chauvet. It seemed as if we used wine as our life's metaphor. In this little world, there was a microcosm; human, artist, science, and nature come together in one special, all-telling bottle.

At the beginning of Eric's search, he was curious about making wine, but he wasn't sure that he would actually become a farmer. "I wasn't passionate about vine growing. I wanted to do something with feelings, and it seemed like being a farmer wasn't about feeling. Now wine—that's about feeling! That could be expressive. Or so I thought."

"What changed?" I asked.

"I met the organic guys from Provence. They explained their philosophy. I saw I could be involved with growing vines with an aesthetic goal. They showed me the beauty of vine growing with nature, not fighting with it. I had been fighting against the nuclear industry for fifteen years. I didn't want that kind of fight anymore."

We arrived at Morgon. This was not a terribly cute town, but a squat one, and the gray skies did not flatter it. Lack of charm be damned, this is where Chauvet hooked up with Lapierre and the resistance against industrial wine bloomed in a small but fierce way.

Domaine Lapierre held enough acreage to fill about five thousand cases a year. The office and winery were certainly bigger than a garage but smaller than the footprint of the Beaujolais Nouveau king, Georges Duboeuf. Eric and I walked into the office and waited among the boxes wrapped up for shipment.

I thought about the times I'd seen Marcel at tastings, electrifying the room with a generous papa sort of aura. His energy was magical. His tasting table was about joy as they all slapped him on the back and clamored for a taste of his new vintage. He had a reputation for staging legendary parties. I had never been to one, but had witnessed some killer hangovers after the Bastille Day bashes.

When Marcel made his entrance this time, I thought that he seemed a little distracted, not making much eye contact. Hands shaken, apologies for my bad French made. His beard closer cropped, his eyes still watery blue and magnified behind his thick eyeglasses, but subdued. He had been dealing with a particularly nasty melanoma.

After the cordial hello, we visited the vineyards, where workers were trimming the vines. We then went to see the way he processed water and waste from the winery—naturally, of course. "One kilo of shit equals three kilos of frogs," he said with a laugh, striking the visit's first spark of mirth. We proceeded to the winery, a spacious barnlike affair with large, old oak fermentation vats. Overhead we saw mystical psychedelic moon murals, painted from the early days of the wine resurrection. In that conservative village of Morgon, they must have caused a stir.

His dimpled wife breezed in and out of our tasting in the small, low-ceilinged cellar. I hadn't seen Marie since February in the Loire at a tasting in the belly of the dungeon of a château. It had been so cold there, we had felt that we were in danger of losing our digits. When she now made it clear that she had prepared lunch and we were to come, there was no argument.

Joining us at lunch was Mathieu, who looked like a trim version of his father with his mother's tousled blond hair. Not every wine-maker was so lucky to have a steady son ready to step in and not screw up the legacy with youthful rebellion. With Mathieu at my right, we commenced with those fat white fingers of asparagus topped off with a mayonnaise as frothy as whipped cream. The spears were so earthy and sweet as parsnip.

In between bites, Marcel held forth about his education at the viticultural school from 1966 to 1969 and about the problem of *piqûre lactique*, an excess of malolactic acid resulting from the over-growth of lactobacilli.

"Before that," he said, "this area was filled with other agriculture. Wine was not the only revenue, so it wasn't necessary to have a vintage every year. If you lost a vintage, you didn't starve. But as monoculture came in, so did an abject fear of piqûre lactique."

Malolactic fermentation usually occurs after alcoholic fermen-tation, and sometimes both types of fermentations take off in the same moment. When malo kicks in first, the wine is left more un-protected and stuck fermentation can result. The next by-product of a stuck fermentation is often vinegar. But because *piqûre lactique* doesn't produce the nail-polish-remover-like aroma of ethyl ac-etate, and sugar can mask the acetic edge at the juice's finish, the problem is particularly noisome. In *piqûre lactique* spoilage may go undetected if you're relying on sensorial clues and not lab tests. Obviously, this is not a desirable situation.

Because of how wines are made in the Beaujolais, they are par-ticularly vulnerable, to boot. The traditional fermentation em-ployed in the region is carbonic maceration, the term used when the enzymatic fermentation starts inside the whole berry, as op-posed to a yeast fermentation in the crushed juice. On the plus side, carbonic maceration produces a lovely, easy, aromatic wine. There is, however, a downside. Carbonic maceration lowers the acidity and leaves the wine even more susceptible to that lactobacillus malady.

"Out of fear," Marcel said, "a recipe emerged: Pick unripe grapes, like at eight percent potential alcohol, so you have a high acid and low pH, more stability but not enough sugar to ferment. So to get the right alcohol, you add as much sugar as you want, then you heated up the juice to start as quickly as possible. You heated it up so hot, you killed everything—all the life—so you had to add yeast. Speed was important. The message is better to chaptalize than to harvest ripe and suffer the consequences."

It took Marcel nine years to become fed up. In 1978, he started to experiment with no sulfur. He had heard that a man was making quite nice wine in that way. Enter Saint Jules.

"La première fois que j'ai rencontré Jules Chauvet, il m'a dit, 'Les deux mamelles du Beaujolais ce sont le sucre et le soufre,'" said Marcel. Everyone laughed. I got most of it except for the key point. I wondered if *mamelles* were some sort of animals.

"Do you know what that means?" asked Eric. When he saw my puzzled look, he continued: "When Marcel first met Chauvet, the scientist said to him that the two tits of the Beaujolais are sugar and sulfur."

Those breasts started the collaboration that rocked the wine world. Virtue triumphant! The British journalist Tim Atkin reported on this ten years later for *Saveur* magazine this way:

> The 1982 vintage provided a rigorous examination of Chauvet's philosophies. It was a warm year, yielding wines naturally low in acidity. All over the region, winemakers

produced volatile, vinegary wines. But Lapierre, guided by Chauvet and Bidasse [Jacques Néauport], came through with his production intact.

This was also around the time that they tried cold carbonic maceration, layering dry ice into the grapes to control the temperature, which helped in defying the renegade bacteria. Marcel also believed that a little *pigeage*, punching down with the feet, the hand, or a tool, or as he did, using a grid to keep the cap of grape crud submerged was enough to prevent that devasting *piqûre lactique*. But simply keeping whole-cluster grapes fermenting in a closed vat was an invitation for trouble.

Natural wine, by whatever name, existed before World War II, before the prevalence of wine schools and the advent of agribusiness that peddled chemicals in the vineyard. Wine quality greatly declined.

"Chauvet hadn't created anything new," Marcel said. "He just returned to an anti-technology way of making wine. Because if you don't love wine, you don't have any motivation to work with nature. And Chauvet loved wine."

Partial (and cold) carbonic maceration created beautiful aromas, and Chauvet had a predilection for aromatics. So until the last years of his life, Chauvet persisted in using carbonic rather than the kind of Burgundian fermentation I had used for my Sagrantino.

All along, the name of Jacques Néauport kept resurfacing. As Chauvet's soldier, Néauport was the keeper of Chauvet's memory and an all-round mysterious guy. After Chauvet died in 1989, it was Néauport who continued Chauvet's theories and research, also working in the Beaujolais with Marcel until 1996.

Even though Chauvet's writings are explicit in his belief that cold carbonic maceration is only appropriate for Gamay on granitic soils, the method spread to limestone, clay, and slate and to other kinds of grapes as well. Chauvet abandoned carbonic maceration in 1984 for his own wines, in the last few vintages, before his death. He even started to use sulfur. So much for Saint Jules.

Marcel took out a large wooden case and selected his cigar, a Cuban, a contemplative punctuation after lunch. "Natural wines should be expressive of terroir and vintage," he said. "But a wine merely without sulfur and not expressing anything is not natural."

"Did you get that?" Eric said.

Yes, I nodded. I got every word of it. It was a profound statement and worth noting again and again.

Marcel said, "People believe that if you make a natural wine, it has to be made in the so-called méthode Chauvet."

Shaking her head of curls, Marie added, "People carry out traditions without knowing where they come from. You're exchanging tradition for dogma."

"Did you get that?" Eric asked me once more.

I didn't mind that Eric was acting like a mother hen, making sure I didn't miss the good bits. I often get about 60 percent of the French, but the missing 40 percent can be devastating. And these statements were at the core of the natural-wine movement and the debates. I wondered if they were telling me in their way about Jacques Néauport, wherever he was. For some reason, I thought he was in Switzerland or in exile. But their comments were very pointed.

The effect of carbonic maceration and the reason for it was the catalyst for my endless conversations with Eric. We talked about the effect of fermentation on wines, the sameness, and how sometimes the desire to make wine without sulfur sacrifices the wine itself. The wines can be slightly fizzy, spicy—think cinnamon—and easy to drink, easy to drink young, often lacking structure, but yes, charming. There are many ways to make wines without sulfur and wines without yeast, but many people, including me, have confused the flavors of carbonic maceration with the true taste of natural wine, instead of just a winemaking choice among many.

We had two more visits in store for the day, all within a stone's throw of each other in town. On the way to Chaudenet, Eric said, "That was very interesting and true, what Marie said about dogma."

"The Chauvet method has become a recipe," I said. "Disciples have accepted the dogma, no? Semi-carbonic maceration, no matter what. No sulfur, no matter what. Chauvetists' wine seems to belong, in taste and style, to a club. I prefer it more than other clubs, though."

"Yes, they can be quite nice, of course. But you know, Alice, I don't like sulfur. In the wine I make from the Fukuoka vineyard, there's none at all. The wine is completely pure, but sometimes you have to add sulfur. Do you know that some people who are very vocal about not using sulfur use a particular enzyme called lysozyme?" He laughed and shook his head. "The people who manufacture that stuff say that carbonic maceration users are their main customers in the wine industry."

"And what do you think about it?" I asked, and of course, he was ready with an answer.

"Its systematic use is totally unacceptable for me, and it is much worse than sulfur or commercial yeasts and bacteria, especially since there are high suspicions of danger for human health. I used it once on 2005 Mâcon, and it was highly efficient. But I somehow managed to lick my fingers during using it, and ended up with the worst tourista of my life. I decided not to use it ever again."

"But what if you had to?" I asked.

Eric told me that this was the beauty of making his wines in one-ton vats, the same size that I used in the Sagrantino project. If he had a problem with *piqûre lactique*, he would just throw the wine out.

"But," I insisted, "what if you would lose a whole vintage of one wine you make?"

He conceded that yes, if that were the case, that is what medicine is for. "Yes, I suppose I would."

The AVN (Association des Vins Naturels) has embedded in its charter a statement about honesty: "A winemaker member of the Association of Natural Winemakers does what he says and says what he does." In the true natural-wine spirit of transparency, Thierry Puzelat, who had at one time worked with Néauport, was very open with me about his enzyme usage. He in fact sometimes does use the enzyme lysozyme to kill off the lactobacteria. "In the 2002 vintage, it was used for all my whites because of maladie de la graisse. My brother Jean-Marie and I use it for a few cuvées of hot vintages like 2005 and 2006 to protect the wine against piqûre lactique. My opinion is that there is no transformation of the wine with it. It's easier to drink than sulfites. But as we don't know how it's extracted from eggs, we don't want to use it for security, not for prevention but only to save a wine, as a last resort."

When we arrived at Domaine Chamonard, Eric stubbed out his cigarette and we walked to the door of the *cuverie* (the area where the vats are stored), which is attached to the Chanudet residence. Joseph Chamonard, who died in 1990, had been the embodiment of the older and truer traditions of the area. He never changed to modernity, so he never had to return. He also never worked with sulfur or other chemicals. Though he was not part of the gang, Chamonard was a reference for them. He and Chauvet were the elders; the young pups like Néauport and Lapierre had the wisdom to recognize the older generation as worth listening to. When people refer to the Band of Five instead of the Gang of Four, they are adding Chamonard. Then Jean-Claude Chanudet from Fleurie married Chamonard's quiet little girl, Genevieve, and the two of them carried on as the old man had.

Blackened, oval wooden casks were lined up against the wall. We sat in the cold room at a long, picnic-type table on which sat bottles of various vintages. Chanudet had prepared for me to taste seven vintages of his wine.

The opposite of dogmatist, Chanudet is ever much the anarchist and will do what he needs to in order to make a sound wine. "As a winemaker," he said, "I believe that you need to give the consumer a good wine. As an anarchist, I believe you let the winemakers do what they want."

He'll decide that, thank you very much. If it happens to be natural, so be it. He had one year that disappeared in a mysterious *piqûre lactique*, and he was not likely to let it happen again.

The Chamonard wines were favorites of Eric's. When he first started to fall for wine, these were his regular purchases, which he bought directly from Monsieur Chamonard himself. I too had noticed these wines, putting stars in the margins of my notes when I first sampled the wines at a Dive Bouteille. I wondered why people whispered to me that Chamonard wasn't really natural. It didn't make a difference; his wines were natural enough for my mouth. The domaine at times practices the honored colder-climate tradition of chaptalization for extending the fermentation so that the wine finishes to dry and has increased alcohol content.

Yes, it was argued that chaptalization was not natural; after all, it is literally an addition. But if someone like Pierre Overnoy from the Jura, one of the more revered winemakers of this genre and an early convert to the natural, feels the need for the process in certain vintages, I will not question his wisdom. I trust certain winemakers in any vintage to make the decision they need to.

Eric and I sat and tasted through a vertical of vintages, and then Genevieve disappeared and returned with a plate of *saucisson* and a black-and-white picture of her father, and tried to explain. "My father believed in modernity," she said. "He loved machines and he loved cars. But he didn't like it when it came to wine."

At the end of our visit, Jean-Claude Chanudet summed it up: "It's not necessarily about natural wine, but why use something when you don't need it? Lately, when it comes to *vin naturel*, you have to justify what you don't do, what you don't add. It's how can you *not* add, yeasts, sulfur, tannin, enzyme. What? You make wine without sulfur? Defend yourself! But the conventional world doesn't have to defend its use of chemicals. That, I don't understand."

Chanudet identifies with *vin naturel* and clutches firmly to his anarchistic identity. He works in a cold-carbonic-maceration way, without *pigeage*. While he isn't against adding sulfur or sugar, he is, in fact, curious about how certain machinery signifies a philosophical hiccup with the spirit of naturally made wine. He brought up, for instance, the possibility of tangential filtration for removing the dead yeasts from the wine.

Once out of earshot, I asked Eric, "But isn't tangential filtration, which is another world for a reverse-osmosis machine, a torture chamber for wine?"

He gave his deep chuckle. "If I say Eric Texier is using tangential filtration, they kill me right away."

There are a few processes that both Eric and I find incomprehensible, and among them is tangential filtration, which is done by a reverse-osmosis machine. Reverse osmosis can be useful if you have stuck fermentation (in fact, it is the only fix for *piqûre lactique*), but as an adjustment, it is squarely contrary to a natural process.

Another "invasive" process in winemaking is thermovinification, which has taken the place of carbonic maceration in much of the Beaujolais and in the southern Rhône. All the thoughtful winemakers I spent time with consider thermovinification a scourge for the region. The process involves heating the juice prior to fermentation to 85 degrees Celsius, for forty-five minutes. Then the wine is treated with enzymes (pectinase), followed by clarification and then inoculation to start fermentation, either with or without seeds. Winemaking through thermovinification is sped up to a few days instead of a few weeks. A wine made in this way cannot be natural.

Eric and I also agreed on our dislike of micro-oxygenation. Sure, you can argue that this technique merely requires the use of oxygen. However, micro-oxygenation is mostly used for tannin management and can grossly change a wine's texture. Aromatic yeasting, over-sulfuring, "new-oaking," or anything else that changes the basic nature of the wine is at odds as well. Those who love wine appreciate the adventure of following the vintage. This is action sport; you should stick your nose in the glass and know something about the vintage. Was it hot like 2003 or 2007? Was it rich like 2009? Were the wines lighter in color such as 2004?

Vin naturel should be naked wine; it is honest, transparent, and sensitive. Whether in a person or in a wine, these are qualities to cherish.

It had started to rain when we arrived in the angular courtyard of the quiet yet grand old house of Jean and Agnes Foillard. We were rewarded with a wild salad filled with wild things: asparagus, scallion, fava, and pea. I am a devout lover of the Foillard wines: deep, lovely, aromatic, structured. Agnes and Jean, both intense and of similar height, sat side by side, looking like serious-visaged brother and sister. The wines were lined up, and we tasted with dinner while I tried to keep my fingers to myself as I eyed the Camembert, dripping like candle wax.

"At the beginning, in 1985," Jean said, "most of my neighbors said it was impossible to make wine without sulfur or yeast."

He heard this standard winemaking recipe over and over, but he was not deterred. There was no problem with fermentation. He tasted Marcel Lapierre's wine and loved it. He became one of the "gang" when made his first natural wine in that year.

Recalling Jacques Néauport, Jean Foillard repeated the refrain: "He was Chauvet's memory." Like Marcel, Foillard also does a little *pigeage*, but unlike Marcel, he does a long maceration, which is obvious, considering the De Beers diamond—worthy faceted structure of the wines. But he started to add 25 ppm of sulfur in 2000, when he lost four thousand of his best *vieilles vignes* to a renegade bacteria. He plucked a bean out of the salad, almost for punctuation, and popped it, gumball-like, into his mouth. "Vin naturel has to be wine first. Its meaning, its place in the world, is transparency."

There is courage in this word *transparency*, and not everyone, even in the natural-wine world, is able to live up to the ideal.

Under the patter of raindrops, Eric drove us back to his place. The forty-five-minute drive gave us time to break down the extraordinary day. I was thinking about Mathieu Lapierre, who was going to follow his father's lead; about Chanudet's daughter, Genevieve, who followed him.

"What did you mean when you said your son will make different wines than you?" I asked him. Eric had often mentioned that his wines aren't natural enough for his son.

"Who wants to make the same thing as his or her parents?" Eric answered rhetorically. "My parents were Bordeaux drinkers. Not me. Plus, remember, my son Martin spent a whole year in Japan. He is very fond of Japanese culture and taste, where hard-core natural and the 'method' are like living gods."

A few years back, Eric, in trying to find out where he belonged in the natural-wine world, worked with cold carbonic maceration, and he too was disappointed. He felt, as I too suspected, the technique masked the terroir. "Anyway, I don't see what is so natural with adding dry ice or carbon dioxide into a vat," he explained.

"Do you know whose idea the dry ice was? Chauvet's or Néauport's?" I asked.

"I really have no idea, but dry ice wasn't readily available when Chauvet started his research," he said.

He now has resumed traditional fermentations on all his Rhône wines but the Fukuoka, on which he uses semi-carbonic maceration, since the grapes are grown in the Beaujolais, as homage to tradition.

For his other wines that are raised for less than thirty months, he adds between 15 and 25 ppm of sulfur at bottling, and for those with over thirty months of aging, most will have no additions. His son Martin has made a small amount of hard-core, no-sulfur, and partial carbonic wines. "He has no trouble selling them," said Eric. "He is clearly in the fashion of hard-core natural. But me, I fall in the cracks. For using twenty milligrams of sulfur, some of the *bars aux vins naturels* in Paris think I am a criminal. In conventional restaurants, because I use twenty milligrams of sulfur on my white Châteauneuf or Condrieu, they tell me that my wines are going to be screwed up because it's too little. For the others, because I use that amount of sulfur, I use too much. I'm industrial for some and hard-core for the others. More and more, the world has no tolerance for gray but needs one to be extreme."

We drove quietly into the cul-de-sac of the Texier house, doors slamming, echoing into the silent night. The hills that sat north were a blur of darkness. The just-clearing skies and the brilliant stars magnified the stillness of one in the morning. Eric started to pat his jacket, and then all pockets of his pants.

"Merde," he said, shaking his keys. He had forgotten the house ones. "Laurence is not going to like this." Who would cherish being woken up in the early morning to let into the house not only your husband, but a stranger, too? I had my first glimpse of Eric as an ever-inquiring, but perhaps absent-minded, rocket scientist. This forgetting-the-key scene had been played out before, which is something else Eric and I had in common.

"Ma cherie," he said as she picked up the phone. The woman looked adorable coming to the door, almost sleepwalking, but she certainly wasn't happy.

Two weeks later, on the summer solstice, I was in Paris and heading to rue de Rivoli, near the Louvre and the Seine, for a tasting. The promoters called it Fabuleux Beaujolais 2009, a tasting through all of the crus. In theory, this was a great opportunity.

I walked into the hotel through the lobby, picked up a glass, and nodded hello to Georges Duboeuf, always elegant in a dove-gray suit. And then I had a go at it.

The 2009 Beaujolais was heralded as the greatest vintage since 1947 because it was rich and round and big. The year was thought to be the one to change everything and bring drinkers back to the region. So what if 2009 was also a year that had plenty of wine-makers all over France in fear of *piqûre lactique*? Taste after taste, my mouth was assaulted with thermovinification and an assortment of banana and bubblegum aromas and flavors. A nuclear bomb went off in my mouth; acidification was out of control in 2009. *Burn, baby, burn*, I heard myself thinking and headed off looking for an ice cube. The region complains that it cannot get a foothold with drinkers. It gets no respect, which is bollocks. After all, there's plenty of respect given to those who make great wine: Lapierre, Chanudet, Foillard, Breton, Thévenet, Lapalu, J-P Brun, Coquelet, Louis & Claude Desvignes, Clos de la Roilette, G. Descombes, and Ducroux, to name a few. A few years ago, suicides tied to an inability to sell wine were contagious in Beaujolais. Why take drastic measures against financial demise when the winemakers could have been proactive and followed the success of those who merely worked more naturally? I suppose the answer is, it's either in your soul or not.

Having cooled off, I returned for more abuse when, to my surprise, over at the Morgon table, I saw Mathieu Lapierre. "Whatever are you doing in this company!" I said as I gave him two kisses.

As he poured for me, he slyly explained that as the day was the twenty-first, it was La Fête de Music. All over France, the streets were lit up and alive with street music. Paris was the best place to be. "A good excuse," he said.

His excuse was my salvation. The wine was filled with baby powder and crushed roses. Yes, 2009 in heft, but Lapierre in elegance.

That night, I too headed out into the street to listen to music. Paris was glowing, even if night didn't fall until 10:30. Still, there was a half moon over the Seine. I aimed for the Left Bank, where the assortment of jazz and vintage music and human voices raising up to the stars on blocked-off streets changed with every few steps. The feeling was joyous and innocent, sexual and raunchy.

I went to an old standby, Fish, on rue de Seine and sat at the bar. I ordered a perfect little Niçoise with marinated *anchois* and creamy, walnut-sized quail's eggs. Some young students traveling before they took on the world and presumed adulthood chatted me up. For the moment, the burn of the sad wines of 2009 was gone, washed down by some enlivened, unacidified Franck Pascal bubbles and a fierce walk back to the Eighth for my pillow.

CHAPTER 6

The Secret World of the Ardèche

It is art that makes life, makes interest, makes importance . . . and I know of no substitute whatever for the force and beauty of its process.
—HENRY JAMES

Except for the cats that wandered in hope for a vole, the southern Rhône hilltop town of Castillon du Gard was silent. I was waiting for Matt Kling and Amy Lillard, American transplants to this area, whom I had met through the usual means these days, the booming wine community on the Internet. I liked what Amy had to say, and she liked what I had to say. There I was in France, propped up near my suitcase, sitting near the one open café, which was adjacent to the church, fascinated by a swaddled man who was probably on his fourth drink of the afternoon and who picked his nose without apology.

Cute, I thought and then pondered the couple who was about to fetch me.

A little over a decade ago, Amy and Matt had hooked up at Kermit Lynch's Eurocentric wine store in Berkeley. She worked. He shopped. They married. Francophones forever, they headed east to Paris in 2001. Why not? After all, they were young, fluent, and free. Even better, Matt's job at Cisco was portable, which is very useful when one wants to expatriot oneself. They settled on Paris. Then, on a road trip to sunny Rhône, they fell for a fixer-upper farmhouse, complete with junk and scorpions, and bailed out on city living for St. Quentin la Poterie, forty minutes directly south of Châteauneuf du Pape. On a rare night when she had visited New York City and we arranged to meet face-to-face for the first time, she explained how they managed to make the decision to move to that extremely tiny little town. "Matt and I do everything on impulse," she said. That meeting was also the first time I heard her signature: a particularly good-natured, self-effacing laugh—a laugh that implied, "The joke's on me."

It took two years for the couple to rehabilitate their old stone house into something habitable. Just when the moldy carpet was ripped out, the walls were fixed, and the gaping holes in the flooring filled, they started their next chapter in peace. Amy had her translation and wine critic work, and Matt had his Cisco work. Life went on for them per usual, until a broker who specialized in vineyards knocked on the door. "He knew we had window-shopped for vines, but all the parcels were ten hectares [about sixteen acres] and were too big. We needed parcels small enough for us to work ourselves." The bank further called the couple's bluff by approving a loan, and 150,000 euros later, they decided to call their winery La Gramière and converted the parcels, about eight acres' worth, into organics.

In some ways, this move was their natural next step. Matt, who has farmers in his family, had once thought of abandoning high tech for an enology degree. Amy once had a commuting relationship between California and the Burgundy vineyards in Gevrey-Chambertin, where she learned to prune and otherwise tend the vines under the tutelage of Madame Bartet, the seventy-five-year-old mother of winemaker Bruno Clair.

"When I was living in France," Amy once told me, "I met Gary Andrus of Pine Ridge [California] and Archery Summit [in Oregon]. He invited me to work harvest with him. I just did not fit in. You can imagine going from Burgundy and a cute little *cuverie* to Pine Ridge stainless steel vats three stories high!"

With these musings, I noticed a car approaching. Seeing that it was Amy and Matt, I walked toward them, wheeling my luggage. After a warm greeting, among much barking of their dogs, I got in and we started driving toward their home. This was my first stop in a two-week tasting marathon. Amy and I had planned to attend La Remise, a rustic event that presented mostly hard-core natural stuff, the next day. She had been struggling with her own wine philosophy, especially how far with natural she should go. She had been to La Remise in the past to find the answer among the faithful, but she had e-mailed me on return, "I just don't get them. A lot are so bad, and taste the same." She complained about the rawness of the material, the unfinished characters, and diffuse tastes. I was curious to taste alongside her, to show her some that I liked and to see how our palates overlapped and agreed or disagreed. Sure, many people don't love some of the crazy natural wines, but there were some delicious examples. I was curious to see if she'd been influenced by her work as a taster for the "French Robert Parker," Michel Bettane. This French wine critic had been vocal about his dislike for natural wine, and to read him, you'd think that all who love the genre would rather be eating browned apples instead of fresh, crisp ones right off the tree.

"Do you want to see our vines?" she asked, turning to me in the backseat, her dog in the rear, slobbering all over me.

"Of course," I answered.

We stopped at one of the parcels right on a main road. We had little time before the sunset. As fiery red streaked the winter sky, we walked on the semifrozen soil between the bare forty-year-old plants—just slightly older than Amy. "This is our own little piece of heaven," she sighed.

The gusty mistral blew through her precise blonde bob as she spoke with such cuddly affection she could have been talking about a new puppy instead of Lauzette, her drought-afflicted, rock-littered vineyards. "It makes such beautiful Grenache," she said. Then she added, with that laugh of hers, "Unfortunately, we blend it all and haven't had enough quantity since 2007 to bottle it on its own!"

Amy and Matt haven't had an easy time of it since they threw off American life and took on the one of vignerons. They're certainly not ready to quit their day jobs. Decreased yields mean they don't have that much wine to sell. One of the reasons for the lack of fertility, Amy said, was the number of years the vines had been mistreated. "When we took over and started in organics, they [the plants] were looking for the chemicals." The two Americans tried to find a farming regime they considered biodynamic, but decided not to buy into it. They cherry-picked techniques and treatments they thought made sense, such as timing vineyard and cellar work to the moon and the use of various tisanes and sprays—chamomile and nettles. But the cow dung in horns? "We use dung, not horns."

"The fertilizer is important, and we actually do use cow dung, but a local option would be better. Do you see a cow around here?" Matt asked by way of explanation. "We eat locally and we want our soil to do the same." When I asked the Santa Rosa–based bio-dynamic consultant Philippe Armenier what they should use for cow shit if they followed biodynamics, he told me that it is best to use that of the local ruminant. But in the end, Matt and Amy decided to find another path to agriculture other than biodynamics. Permaculture, a kissing cousin of Fukuoka's "doing as little as possible" approach, appeals to them, not out of laziness but because of naturalness. They are also investigating the uses of ground stones to adjust the soil. "We decided to try it and got micronized basalt dust," said Amy. "Last year, I put two hundred kilograms per hectare on one of our parcels, and we noticed that the leaves looked greener and it suffered less from drought."

We left the barren vines, and within seconds, Amy was fishing around in her fridge. She emerged with a champagne and popped the cork while Matt immediately started to roll out pasta dough for ravioli. The house had rough-hewn stone walls, rustic furniture, and a sheltered courtyard. Next to a roaring fire, we toasted to whatever—new friendships and wine.

"This all looks like a Peter Mayle *A Year in Provence* fantasy," Amy said in front of the Lacanche eight-burner stove, which I'd kill for, "but really, it's not!"

Amy protested way too much. The place was gorgeous. So what if it had once been riddled with crappy carpet, flaky green paint, and mildew? Promising to be back in two minutes, I carried my bag up the stone steps to my room. My teeth needed brushing, and my face needed water after the long trip down from Charles de Gaulle. There I was, looking into my weary face, wondering why

I was tied to my tenement apartment in New York. Adventure called out to me, but I still stayed on Elizabeth Street, walking up my five flights, hiding behind a keyboard, escaping for wine tastings and vineyard visits in the United States and in France, but a home and a different life escaped me. I began to wonder if, instead of living life, perhaps I just wrote about the lived lives of others.

Champagne waited for me downstairs, and I flicked the bedroom light, and there on the wall, past the bed but in jumping distance of it, I saw something dark. It was an odd shape, like an embryo with a cleft palate.

I sneaked up on the critter to investigate and saw a perfect miniature, a familiar-looking arthropod with pincers. "Uh, Amy?" I called down, knowing I was interrupting her bubbly. "Could you, um, come here?"

I heard her groan, "Uh-oh!" and then she sprinted up the steps, sensing that something was more the matter than my tone revealed. "What's the matter?"

Backing up and then approaching the speck on the wall, I pointed.

"Oh my God," she cried, mortified. She knocked down the miniature scorpion.

"Amy, it has to die!" I said and stepped on it.

She placed her hand over her mouth and said, "I am so embarrassed!"

"Amy it's not a pack of mice or cockroaches! You live in the country."

"At harvest, they're all over the place; you have to be careful when you put your shoes on in the morning and when you cut the grapes. That aside, we've never seen one in the vineyards or in a shoe."

"Remind me not to work harvest," I said with a smile. "I'll stick with the northern climates!"

"Oh, it's not so bad. It's not even as bad as a bee sting," she said.

After the wine and the ravioli, I was finally rewarded with bed. I scrutinized the sheets first. Secure that there was nothing lurking there to bite me, I climbed in. The moral of the story is, if it looks like a scorpion, then it is a scorpion.

In the morning, before the tasting, we took a detour into the tank room in the old garage. Amy scrambled up a ladder to the top of one of the seventy-year-old cement fermenting and *élevage* tanks.

"I didn't know if I wanted to make wine in California," she said. "Ah, no, I don't think I could have. I don't see the point of making wine if you haven't grown the grapes. And who could afford land there! And where? I don't drink Californian wine. Then there's the actual price of the bottle of wine itself. I want to make wine that I can afford to buy. We couldn't have done this in California, where a vigneron doesn't really exist."

I nodded my head. I understood. It was just the way I felt with my inchoate Sagrantino experience. Making wine from vines you tend yourself must be a much more intense emotional experience. What Amy and Matt are doing—ripping out the vines, replanting, living with the vintage—is essential. Otherwise, it is just a job. This was not the case with their La Gramière.

Their first vintage was 2005, Amy said. "It was a wonderful vintage, but never having made wine, who knows what to think! It was our child, and I couldn't judge it objectively. The whole thing ended up great, but it started out a nightmare. It was like you're pregnant and all of a sudden, your water breaks, you say 'Oh shit,' and nothing's ready. We didn't have our tanks or electricity until the day before harvest. Stress was really high. Our family was here to help. Guess what? They didn't speak French. Matt and I had the biggest fight we ever had on the last day we brought the grapes in. In front of everyone."

She said that inside the winery, her consultant enologue (a consultant that most rural winemakers without in-house laboratories hire to do testing) used scare tactics. These enologues go by the book. "He told such horror stories, I think it's his way of trying to get us to agree to anything. When the wine didn't go through malo right away, the enologue wanted us to put a heating coil in the tank. I was, like, 'But it will caramelize the wines!'"

In the end, they went ahead without the coil and the wine proceeded through malolactic fermentation all by itself. The wine transformed into something rich and lovely.

"Before we took on the land," she said, "a lot of winemakers said ninety percent is done in the vineyard, and if you did the work, it's easy—we shouldn't worry. That is so absolutely not true. I threw two batches of rosé away because I refused to yeast them. I wanted to be natural. You have to be willing to make mistakes if you want to go the natural route."

Poor Amy and Matt. There is terrific outside pressure to make a technologically correct wine, but they had some built-in defenses. "After all of those years working with the terroir-driven wines that Kermit Lynch imported," she said, "yeasting my wine or adding shit in it was not going to be our path." Of more concern was the use of sulfur and the stigma attached to using it. "All the cool kids are into sans soufre, and if you want to be cool . . ." said Amy, her voice trailing off.

Even here, all roads lead to Marcel Lapierre. Amy had been working for Lynch when the "Beaujolais Band" he imported toured the United States, and it was she who ferried them around, learned their philosophy, and fell in love with their spirit.

As Amy climbed down from the top of the tank, she dripped some of the 2009 into the glass and let out a nervous laugh. "This was a difficult year," she said. Low acid and high pH make for a lot of instability and, as Eric Texier warned, set up the scenario for lactobacillus infection to ruin the entire production. "I think you'll like this," she said, "because you like stems." She was right. I happen to believe that especially in hot years, the use of stems usually regulates the wines and helps to create interest as well as freshness.

"The stems were accidental. We loaned out the de-stemmer, and then all of a sudden, we had grapes! So we pressed off the stems two weeks later. But now, I'm thinking stems are the way to go. Maybe it's the reason we didn't have the difficulty others did? But what do we know—we're just a couple of white kids from Denver and Minneapolis," she said with a shake of her bob and that cascade of a laugh, and we walked back to the house.

After saying good-bye to Matt and the dogs, I flung my bags in the car, and we drove off to La Remise outside the city of Nîmes. I could tell Amy was nervous. "Why?" I asked her.

"Oh, they're going to ask me about my wine and assume I'm one of them."

"Let's talk about this," I said. "I don't understand why you're so apologetic."

"Isn't that funny?" She looked wistful as she said, "I don't know, Alice, but in France, this whole natural movement is kind of a cult thing. So you're like me. You do your best; you make your wine with nothing, and you add sulfur, and you get booted out of the club. And that eats at me, because we're totally natural except for sulfur. Yet, sometimes I just want to be in the club!"

That special *sans soufre* club was definitely where the cool kids of any age hung out. This was the crowd for those who longed to be of age in Woodstock or who were too young to be part of the civil rights effort. It was for those who saw the Chicago Seven trial as evening entertainment and for those who knew that the 1960s and early 1970s was a time when values and ideas and music mattered. It was also for those who simply believed that the wines were better without sulfur.

Not only that, on a hedonistic note, this natural-wine arena was about community. For people with an anarchistic bent and who loved to drink with like-minded individuals, that world was for them.

I understood Amy's desire to want entry and acceptance. She looked to me as if I held a place on the inner circle. The joke? It wasn't true. Whether the group was inclusive or not, I was a kid sitting in the corner of the party. There are circles around the circles, and I didn't feel myself on the innermost circle at all. God knows what these people thought of me, the short red-haired American reliving my youth, politics, and passions through these wines. I saw her as someone who could be one of their intimates. After all, she used as little sulfur as Eric Texier did, and she was beautifully transparent about it. From where came the insecurity? Were the hard-core sulfur people really so exclusive?

There was barely a place to park, but once we were successful, we walked to the hall where the tasting was in progress. Five euros bought us each a wineglass. Overwhelmed by hunger, we first went in search of food. Our luck, it was five minutes until 2 P.M., and in France, that is the end of food until dinner. Sadly for us, many people were finishing off the last of their oysters, slurping down the mammoth Utah Beach bivalves in a way that always reminded me of sucking on rocks. We scrounged and came across the world's most delicious, dense cookies and headed into the energetic tasting. Many familiar faces manned their little tables, hawking bottles of their latest vintages.

The Italians were there. The Catalans were represented. I almost walked on by, but then I made eye contact with Laureano Serres, whose wine label is Mendall. Courtesy meant I had to stop. Serres was unshaved and reddened, as if he had been up all night, which he probably had. His gentle face, with a once-broken nose, seems to have lived hard. Amy and I tasted; thankfully, we loved the whites especially. And the reds he had that day were made without carbonic maceration. I liked the wines so much, I promised I would come to see him. "In June?"

"Why not?" he said. "With pleasure."

Next I had to drag Amy over to the mysterious man in the corner who fused Baryshnikov grace with Prague grunge. To top it off, he looked good in a kilt. I'd been entranced with Andrea Calek's wines since the year before, when a Belgian importer had seen me leaving the organic-wine fair Millésime Bio in nearby Montpellier, France, and asked, "Did you taste the crazy Czech's wine from the Rhône?" I had gone over to a very disheveled man with an asymmetrical haircut. I wasn't expecting much. Then I tasted his wine labeled Babiole. The Belgian whispered to me, "Carbonic."

"No!" I said. "How? There's none of that fermentary kind of flavors, no cinnamon? I just get straight élevage." The great mystery why that wine did not taste carbonic—why it had depth and structure—has been on my mind ever since.

"OK," I now said to Amy, "try these, and tell me all crazy natural wines taste the same."

Andrea had fashioned a new look for himself: a Mohawk that pushed out from the side of his head. We approached his table and said hello. He recognized me, mostly, I imagine, because we have e-mailed from time to time over the past year. I introduced Amy, and then he took off on the tasting.

Amy was impressed. "You're right. These don't taste carbonic," she said.

I suspected the lack of carbonic taste in these wines was because they had a longer *élevage* than most. But I wasn't sure. Then and there, I promised to come and visit him as well, in June. As we left, Amy said, "You're just piling those visits up. First Laureano, now Andrea."

"Will you come with me?" I asked.

"To Spain, nope. But this guy? Hell yes," she said. And with that, she went back home. The moon was in the right position, and she had to prune her vines.

Five months disappeared in a blink, and once more, I was jet-lagged in Amy and Matt's house. This time, I went to bed without a scorpion visitation.

The next morning, Amy and I headed to Valvigneres, the secret little town in the Ardèche. When you search for "Valvigneres" on-line, you mostly come up with a lot of nothing, not even wine. What you find is the restaurant and La Tour Cassé, the village inn. If you know what you're looking for, you can also discover that quite close to Valvigneres is Alba la Romaine, the ancient Roman capital. But for all intents and purposes, except for a clutch of hard-core makers of natural wine and La Tour Cassé, which has an insider wine list, the place doesn't seem exist.

We arrived at our one-block destination an hour and a half late. Our meeting place was in front of Gerald Oustric's Le Mazel Winery. I got out of the car and knocked on the locked and weathered plank board door. Nothing. I checked my phone. No service. "Great," I muttered. I walked around to see if I could rev up some cell reception when finally, a small bar flared on my iPhone.

"Two seconds," Andrea said when I reached him by phone. And in two seconds, his truck, a wreck of a thing, appeared and rumbled to a stop. A threadbare wolfhound hopped out of the truck and rushed to sniff us with her wet, pointed-as-an-arrow nose.

Andrea slinked toward us like an exotic lemur. He wore sarong-like pants. His smooth, bare chest shimmered with beads of sweat. Lean, tanned, and frankly sexual, he was fresh from the vines, his head done up in a black scarf affair that trailed down his back. His wraparound sunglasses gave him that angry edge, less so when I noticed they were missing an earpiece. What, I wondered, do people around this rural and hidden area think of this man, an outsider who makes such beautiful wines?

What fascinated me about this particular punkish winemaker (other than the terrible fact that I never have grown out of my bad-boy phase) is what compelled him to leave Prague for France and start making wine in the Rhône. Not just any wine, but this natural stuff. It's not as though he came to America to find his fortune. It's more as if he left Prague to join a band of bandits. And what's more, he backs up his compelling wine with a compelling history, which he told us on the way to his vines.

Cigarette dangling out the window, Andrea rattled the biography that started with his birth in 1970 and his life growing up under Communism. He said he made his first wine when he was sixteen, from currants. "My grandmother's recipe, without added sulfur but with lots of sugar. It was drinkable but very hard for the head."

He read Baudelaire and yearned to go to Southern France and smoke hashish, which is what he did as soon as he had his first two-week leave from his stint in the army. "I went to Marseille and didn't want to come back. I wanted to stay at least another week. I asked my mother to tell the military that I was sick and wasn't sure when I'd be well enough to travel. My mother, she's very special. She said, 'Ondra, fuck you.' Then she called my superiors and told them her son had gone AWOL. The army was looking for me everywhere, and they were looking for me when I got home."

When the Wall came down, he returned to France. He started to smoke Gitanes, and while they took, the hashish did not but the wine did. Enter *vin naturel*.

By the end of the decade, he was in winemaking school in the Macon. I could see it coming before he told me. Mâcon was the same school that Marcel went to. I wasn't a bit surprised when he told me he took an apprenticeship with Le P'tit Max—Max Breton, one of the original gang. Chauvet was already dead, but Néauport was living nearby in the Ardèche and still flitted in and out of Villié-Morgon.

"So you knew Néauport?" I asked

"Of course! He consults with Gerald. Sometimes I ask him questions."

"You're kidding! He's right near here?" I asked, not believing it. I thought he was in Switzerland.

"Quite close."

In fact, it turns out that Néauport might have been the patron saint of Valvigneres. While his name had mostly disappeared from the rest of France, it was alive in this Ardèche town. He was part of that secret world, and while Andrea's wines didn't taste like carbonic maceration, Gerald Oustric's did. Gerald was one of Néauport's remaining clients.

I remembered the theory that I had started to formulate a few months back on a humid, warm night in October. I had locked up my bike to the scrappy scaffolding outside Ten Bells, the Lower East Side den of unmessed-with wine. It was midnight, and people were thick on Broome Street, but inside, candles flickered invitingly. I scored a seat for myself at the squared-off horseshoe of a bar, next to a decanter being filled with Dard & Ribo's K, a Marsanne that two guys, in from San Francisco for the Louis/Dressner wine tasting earlier, had just ordered. Dard & Ribo, who make wine in Crozes-Hermitage, are favorites, and before I drooled, they kindly passed me a glass. I slipped out of ennui and was glad to have gone social. Mid-sip, I was rushed by my favorite Charnay-dwelling winemaker, the ever-thinking vigneron Eric Texier, who ran over to me and urgently asked, "What's the guy's name?"

"Come on, Eric, give me some sort of clue!" I demanded.

"Néauport!" he answered.

"Jacques!" I delivered. I wasn't senile yet.

With a slap to his head as if to say, *How could I forget*, Eric ran away to continue a conversation elsewhere in the mosh pit. Taking my glass, I followed him to where he was holding court and said, "You just can't invoke that name and run away, and not tell me why." I knocked back another gulp and listened.

"Remember, Chauvet never advocated only making wine without any sulfur. And he only advised cold carbonic maceration with Gamay on granite soils. The semi-carbonic maceration was to Chauvet the best way to express granitic terroirs from the Beaujolais. From only the Beaujolais. He even wrote that applying it to the Grenache grape was heresy! Néauport, on the other hand, was advocating the cold carbonic maceration for all terroirs and all grapes. Yet, Chauvet never said anything about the use of sulfur as a stabilization agent when all fermentations are over and, furthermore, for the bottling. By the way, there is evidence that Chauvet always bottled with sulfur."

Heresy in some worlds, I thought.

"If one takes the time to read Chauvet's work," Eric said, "you find everything and its contrary. At one point, he is enthusiastic about yeast selection, and then he is not anymore. Same for carbonic. Saying that Chauvet was advocating carbonic for any wine is really a way of twisting his work. Same for the use of SO_2. My understanding is that he was a 'why do it if you don't need it' kind of guy."

"So you think that the hard-core man was Néauport?" I asked.

He nodded his head, "Possibly."

"So, Chauvetists really are Néauportists!" I exclaimed.

Néauport. The name was whispered about in Beaujolais. My French publisher, Jean-Paul Rocher, had once published Néauport's books as well. He had advised me, "Go and find out for yourself."

It all started to become a little clearer though still fuzzy: the method, the carbonic, the cinnamon, the spice, the perfume in the wine. It came from Néauport's influence. "I have to meet him," I said.

"Of course," Eric said. "Why not?"

Remembering this conversation now, I knew I couldn't take more time on this trip. I had to get to Spain. This search was going to take a minor fortune, but I vowed I'd come back and get to the bottom of it all. Another trip to Ardèche was in my future.

We took a short ride to a barn, which sat in back of a swimming pool. The bronzed, bikini-clad woman we walked past was impossible to ignore. With Andrea making an appropriate comment about her, we walked into the warm shed area holding his fiberglass tanks, where he makes about twenty-five wines, most of which he does merely for experiment. And then we were on to his Grande Arnaque, the big joke, a fat and slutty Syrah he calls *une belle pute*, beautiful whore.

During our barrel sampling, again I just couldn't understand. "Why don't they taste like those perfumed carbonic tastes and aromas?" The wines burst open my observation that carbonic maceration wines taste the same. It was very difficult to understand.

He said that every day, he drains off the juice from the tank and places it in another tank. The juice then continues its alcoholic fermentation as if it were a white wine, without the stems and seeds and skins. Still, the wine was extracted, as if it had been trodden a little bit, or punched down, or had the cap submerged. I was completely stumped with the conflict between my palate and what he was telling me. My reality was challenged.

Then Andrea gave me the "it's not me, it's the terroir" bullshit. But he knew he was bullshitting, because he put that damned wink at the end for punctuation. Perhaps it's what comes of growing up in Communism; you learn to be secret, but not without a fierce sense of irony. "Anyway," Andrea said, "Sometimes I think."

"No pigeage?" I asked.

He claims not to do any *pigeage* or cap submerging. I have to say, I still am not totally sure I believe him, though I can't imagine why he would mislead me, other than to have some sport.

"Why? I asked.

"I'm lazy," he answered.

"You don't use sulfur?"

"As a rule, no. But if a wine needs it, I use it."

"The Grande Arnaque," he says, putting some of the 2009 in our glasses, "I put in sulfur. If I need it, I put in one gram. What I do know is that I won't go to hell if I use it. Sulfur is to sleep well. If you need to sleep well, you use it."

From my end of things, it didn't look as if he really needed to sleep. He had boundless energy. Or perhaps if he does need peace of mind, he needs to add the sulfur. But one gram? It is often said that sulfur allows a winemaker peace of mind—that the wine will be safe from unwanted organisms. After all, the substance is an antiseptic, a safeguard for the wine. But one gram of sulfur is far too little and would do nothing at all. It would take at least fifteen grams for him to be able to sleep without worry.

Andrea lived in a 1970s sort of trailer on the Oustrics' property, in back of the vines. Very soon, he said, he would start to move out to the middle of his vineyards in Saint Pierre, but for now, we took our seats at a white plastic table in his trailer while he put on the sound track for *Amélie* and brought out more wines. With the accordion in the background, I asked his definition of natural wine. He shrugged and said in his edged English, "Nothing added, nothing taken away."

He went on: "It's an ideal, a philosophy, and it's not always attainable. Natural wine is more of an ideology now, more a feeling and that is what is interesting. You cannot make a truly natural wine in every year. Natural wine is quite easy and quite easy for me. Here's the thing: I don't know why put something in the wine if the wine doesn't need it."

We were surrounded with beauty; there was no plumbing on site. I went in search of the prettiest, most sheltered place to squat. With one pair of jeans for three weeks, there was no way I was going to risk a dribble. It was so peaceful there. Andrea is a bit of a wild man, certainly one of a kind, a character driven by a vision, by the wind, and he reminds me of the saying "crazy . . . like a fox." He was not an idealist at all, and yet he wasn't driven by a common concept of capitalism, even though he hated his Communist upbringing. He was a puzzle, and so were these wines.

I returned to the plastic table and the next bottle to taste Chatons de Gardes. It was a Syrah. And this guard kitten of a wine had a puppy breath finish, something that can be particular to low-sulfur wines, like it or not. This is where sulfur could tighten up and refocus the wine. But still, with its sappiness and threads of patchouli, it worked. He next pulled out his Punk Czech, his homage to Domaine Peyra—a wine that was delicious and made in a classic Chauvet style, or was that a Néauport style? It was light and barely colored and had those spicy, floral aromas as if it was a trademarked *vin naturel*. The very kind that Eric's son Martin had no trouble selling. But this wine was very different from Andrea's *vin de garde*.

Nightfall comes late near the solstice. The light was a sheer silky blue. The mosquitoes were not quite out yet. The others were waiting for us at the long table in the garden of La Tour Cassé. Among them were the Rembrandt-looking Gerald Oustric, the Aramis-like Jerome Jouret of the nearby Domaine Les Clapas, and two women I saw as Andrea's nymphs, who helped him in the vineyards. One of them, Virginie, sat next to me and wanted to practice her English. She took my pen and started to scribble something in my notebook:

> There are two groups. 1) you have money 2) you don't have money. What's the difference???? The indifference of course, or the independence, of course?

She looked quite satisfied with herself. I was scratching my head over that one. But, of course, this group did not have money. I didn't, either. This we had in common. I have my independence. Of course. So did they, and neither one of us had indifference. I found myself thinking, *Perhaps I should pick up and move to Valvigneres.*

The nymphs left to create a little party on Gerald's rooftop, and the rest of us, about ten altogether, stayed back and ate and drank and smoked. I indulged, because why the hell not. The night fell, and Amy, who had given up the thought of driving home, and I decided to spend the night. We relaxed and poured some more wine. In addition to Andrea's wines, we were loving Les Clapas. Then the fun started. Gerald asked Amy, as they all do at some point, "Why didn't you bring your wines?"

She blushed in the dark and said she wasn't *vin naturel*, because she used sulfur—even though, at this point, her own idea of what is natural wine had changed. She realized that with her organic viticulture and nothing added in the winery except some sulfur, in low doses, she qualified in every way, except in her own mind.

But how much sulfur did she use? they asked.

"Very little," she answered. I could hear the guilt. The guilt was still there. Then the conversation turned to farming and the connection between natural and organic and how they intertwine. The French language was going way too fast for me, but I heard the product name Roundup being brandished like a sword as the emotions heated up. This weed-control chemical is a particular bugaboo for me because so many people say to me, "I'm organic except for Roundup."

Amy was very upset. "There are people I know who make a supposedly natural wine and use Roundup. And that's more natural than my wines, because I use sulfur?"

The table exploded. This all reminded me of the arguments between my grandfather and uncle about the Talmud and what to do if the cow falls in a rut on Shabbos. Gerald brought up Saint Jules and reflected that to not need science, you had to be a great scientist. Andrea started to raise his voice about the importance of organics. The innkeeper proudly brought out bottles of wines from her daughter who had moved to just outside Rome, where she made wine. Two bottles came out. One bottle, one of the few cold carbonic wines I had ever tasted from Italy was delightful, of course. But even though the natural way has been exponentially spreading in Italy since 2006, this was my first taste of Italian wine made in the Néauport method.

That night, after they had all left and Amy had gone to sleep, I stayed behind to speak to Gerald. He speaks not a word of English, but was extremely patient with my French, and somehow we managed to converse for the next hour. He had read my book; it seems as if the whole village had. I was surprised and felt exposed, as that book laid my life out in a way that was perhaps too vulnerable. However, the takeaway from that night was that Amy should bring her wine and not worry about the sulfur. "We all do what we have to do make our wine safe for the world," Gerald said.

CHAPTER 7

That Obscure Object of Desire: Real Wine in Spain

It is impossible to produce natural wines, if the person who produces it is not natural.

—JOSKO GRAVNER

In the short two decades after Franco's death, Iberia's Old World wine went new. Some loved the resulting modern wines. The marketing arm of Spanish wines shouted the affection on their website: "The transformation of the image and quality of Spanish wines during the last quarter of the 20th century has been truly remarkable. During this period, a group of hard-working pioneers began to introduce and apply new wine producing techniques being used elsewhere." But others, like me, took such statements as heresy, not nationalism. We saw Spain as having sacrificed preexisting expressions. Many old vines and varieties were saved, but there was also a huge planting of new international varieties such as Chardonnay, Pinot Noir, Cabernet, and Merlot. It didn't matter whether the grapes were old or new, indigenous or foreign—all of them were made in woody, overextracted styles at the expense of terroir. In short, Spanish wine was a disaster.

That was before American-based, Spanish-born boy genius José Pastor decided to be a wine importer when he grew up. He and I met through a bottle of wine. By chance, I tasted a Rioja he imported, Bodegas Peciña. The wine grabbed my attention for its unabashed sense of place. I went to Spain and visited the Peciñas and their vines. Upon my return, José, who is based in California, called me up. The next time he was in New York City, we met. We tasted. We talked. We made friendship. I was touched by the young Valencian man's pride in his country and how he wanted to champion what was lost. I wondered: With his help in developing a thirsty market in America for wines that were not "espoofulated," could the wines of Spain be saved? Oh, if only!

I found another morsel of hope at the 2010 Millésime Bio, the international organic wine tasting in Montpellier, France. There, a like-minded, tow-headed Danish importer whispered in my ear, "Do you ever miss Albariño?" He could have just as easily evoked nostalgia by saying, "Want some Ecstasy?"

He led me to Todd Blomberg, a slightly chubby man, snug in his rag sweater, with silky brown hair that fell into his spectacles. His wines? Spectacular.

Todd was initially suspicious of me. I was just any other schnook at his tasting table. I have no idea what turned the page for him, but by the time he poured his second wine for me, he let me in on his fairy tale.

Living in California, he had thought he was all alone in the world until he fell in love with a woman from the greenest part of

Spain: Galicia. She was sent to him, he said, like an angel on his birthday. And like an angel, she carried him away on her shoulders to her country, where he decided there was one course in his life to follow, that of the vigneron. He hitched up with the winery Sucesores de Benito Santos, became a partner, and, by 2003, was given free rein. He slaved away like a maniac, doing what they said could not be done in the area: grow organically. And he did what they said he couldn't do: make wine without adjuncts or without removing the acidity—the region's norm. He didn't change the wine's aromas by using aromatic yeasts. When he told me that in his attempt to make wine without sulfur, he used a butter churner, I knew he was just the kind of nutcase I had to get to know. I needed to see this churner for myself.

Lured by the promise of *maybe*, I traveled to Spain twice in 2010 to find me some wine heroes. The first time was a few weeks after meeting Todd Blomberg in February. I was pacing in my Santiago de Compostela hotel lobby, contemplating spending the day in nearby Galician vineyards in northwest Spain, specifically in his Rías Baixas area, which hugged the Atlantic coast. The forecast included the threat of a monsoon. José was to meet me, and I doubted his flight could land in the high winds, but then a text came in from the young maverick: "Will arrive from Valencia. See you at Rodri's."

Excellent.

I resumed my pacing, but not for long, interrupted as I was by the man I waited for. Looking windblown, Todd walked briskly into the lobby. I looked at the frenzied man and thought, *This Californian—a fellow Jew, no less—expatriate to Spain, is one of the saviors of the country's devastated wines, in this case, the disabused Albariño grape?* The world was a strange place.

The grape's home, the Rías Baixas, was a baby among Spain's appellations (in Spain, an appellation is called Denominación de Origen, or DO). The DO Rías Baixas was only established in 1986. Varieties planted here other than Albariño are Loureira Blanco, Treixadura, Caiño Blanco, Torrontés, and Godello, but Albariño accounts for almost 90 percent of the vines. In 1987, there were only 568 acres of vines, but by 2010, the number had ballooned to 9,600. Since that time, the region's identity had been stolen, sent to the plastic surgeon for reformation. Gallo is one of the big foreign names that have heavily invested. For some misbegotten purpose, people started to use technology to transform the quiet-smelling grape, angular and mineral with superfresh acidity, into an aromatized screamer. It had also been stripped of its acidity by deacidification. The wine, which I had always considered the Muscadet of Spain, had been transformed into a forgettable, sugary lemonade. But Blomberg's was the real deal.

Blomberg's car tires pressed into the mud. Climbing out of the car and stepping into the vineyard, both of us sank into the wet sponge of the soil. As we slipped through the vine's rows, the sweet smell of wild mint and thyme seemed to squeak under our feet. His terroir was fascinating, intertwined red and pink granite, sparkling like Tinker Bells in the vineyard. We took refuge from the rain, running inside to the winery. Like Pellegrini's, this was a functional, unromantic prefabbed bunker. The aisles were lined with gleaming stainless tanks—this is not the tiniest operation. One wooden fermenter was snuggled into a corner, and there, sitting in the middle aisle, was a very industrial, very curious electric butter churner.

"You weren't kidding me!" I said as I walked over to the squat cylindrical machine. Blomberg lifted its metal cover. Inside was a thick liquid the color of clay slip.

Fermented wine throws behind crud, the dead yeast cells called the gross lees. The wine gets drained off and placed in another vessel like a barrel. But there is still more sediment left behind, the more delicate fine lees. These nourish and protect a wine during its *élevage*. Sometimes they get stirred; the French word for this is *battonage*.

Before bottling, instead of ditching the fine lees, Todd removes them and then plunks them into the butter churner, retaining them for addition into the next vintage. How does this figure into nothing added or taken away? I'm not sure, but they are the grapes' own spawn and they do settle out. In a sense, this is another version of allowing the nitrogen-rich lees to nourish and protect the wine, and it is the method that, he believes, will allow him to bottle some wines without any sulfur. It's his wine. He gets to do what he wants to it.

He encouraged me to sniff. I was expecting lee-like earth, dirt, and funk. "It's floral!" I said, completely stunned.

"See, I told you," he said, a little pleased with himself.

"But why all of this effort to make a wine without sulfur?" I asked.

"To me," he said, "making natural wine is something that comes back to my passion for the kitchen and cooking." He then cited his desire, butter churner aside, to use as little intervention as he can. "Wine without sulfur is a dream," he said and then turned pouty. "But no one understands these wines."

Obviously, he was with the wrong American importer, and I was going to fix that.

At the day's end, we ended up at the winery owned by Rodrigo Mendez, whose wines are made by Raúl Perez, a famous consultant. Perez's thumbprint is so pressed into the wines in that area, people joke that Galicia is, in fact, DO Raúl Perez.

I was surprised to see the vat room cluttered with people, including the famed winemaker and the one friendly face I was expecting. "José!" I cried and went over to greet the newly bearded man with a chunky camera around his neck. I soon introduced my new friend Todd to José, hoping to play matchmaker for a wine and an importer.

After tasting through the wines we were off on an adventure. "Mrs. Feiring," José said to me, using what I can only imagine is a term of affection, "we're going to La Signora." Seems as if Rodrigo Mendez loved old vines and had found some incredible ones to rent, in some older woman's backyard.

These Galicians, all on the young side of forty, traveled in packs. Three cars of us caravanned, and twenty minutes later, we pulled up to a stone house that in the bluing light looked like a Catskill farmhouse. Through the house's lace curtains, we could see the family licking up the bits of the inevitable Sunday pig. After obtaining permission from La Signora, our little parade went double-file to the backyard, where in the place of a lawn was a vineyard built on rustic terraces. The sun was going down fast, and the night would be moonless. My eyes strained to take in this dramatic site of hundred-year-old Albariño and Caiño vines, their wood pulled up about six feet in the air, onto the traditional granite square poles. The vine arms stretched out on the top wires, like laundry hanging out to dry. In the summer, when they were in full leaf, the plants would provide a shade canopy. The fruit would hang pendulously above, far from the damp ground so that the berries could air-dry in the mold-provoking climate.

La Signora's daughter entered the garage. She completed her sturdy, peasant look with an inviting smile. With a plastic tube placed one end in her mouth, the other in the bunghole of an ancient barrel, she siphoned out some red liquid to distribute in our clunky glasses. The red was a Caiño. It had a Loire Valley Pineau d'Aunis, sort of Red-Zinger-meets-pepper quality. The daughter was talented and, in my opinion, the region's next star, yet she has no aspiration to make wine commercially. Slipping my arm through his, I whispered to José, "That's the wine you should import."

José clamped his plump lips together, widened his hazel eyes, and nodded vigorously. We both had seen an angel.

It was a different story back at Rodri's winery and vat room when we tasted his version from the same Caiño vineyard. All of the charm and personality had been erased, into a clean, modern, direct, and uninteresting taste. The wine was neutered. We became convinced that the best winemaker in Rías Baixas was not Rául Perez but the La Signora dynasty. Finally, Blomberg had to get home. The pack of Galicians, José, and I were off to dinner, and I waited to see if my wine matchmaking had produced any chemistry.

A few days later, I left Todd to go home and deal with the monsoons of 2010, which seemed not to stop until mid-June, the month I would return to Spain. But this time, I was to land on the other side of country, the sunnier more eastern coast, where a wine revolution was under way. With any luck, I was going to wade deep into it.

The morning after the EcoSostenible conference I had been attending, I walked out to the parking lot of my hotel and waited in a corner of the shade for a man in a truck. The sun was as brilliant as a halogen lamp. *Gosh,* I thought, *where is that nice cool glass of Todd's Albariño when I need one?* Instead of drinking, I mulled over the past few days filled with talks, ideas, and even propaganda.

BASF, the chemical company giant with $3.6 billion in sales (and Monsanto's partner), was one of the presenters and cosponsors. It promoted its efforts as crop protection and had just debuted Amflora, the transgenic potato. The presenter projected a snappy PowerPoint talk about fuel consumption. According to BASF, an apple out of season shipped to Spain from Chile was more eco-minded than a local and organic apple in season. I didn't have to raise my hand; half the audience was ready to jump on him. What he failed to address is which fruit had better nutrition and taste. Why did we need out-of-season apples, anyway? There, under the guise of an organic and sustainable conference, was a corporate advocate for chemical farming.

During one event dinner, I sat next to Miguel Torres, a veteran winemaker in the Penedès. Ever since he had seen the Al Gore film *An Inconvenient Truth*, he had been on the reduced-carbon-footprint trail. Also, he had become viewed as a champion in organic viticulture. He advised me to choose his favorite dish, the chickpea stew, and then segued into his misgivings. Perhaps, he suggested, organic was not so great after all: "You use a lot of fuel for the tractors because it takes so much more physical work." What if, he mused, he could make one pass with a tractor to spray one chemical instead of the several passes it often takes with organic? What if?

One of the best responses came from Eric Texier, in the Rhône. Since Eric went organic, he doubled his fossil fuel consumption. Yet, he said, "Organic growing is like democracy: a bad system, but the least bad of all the systems I know for growing vines and making wines from their fruits that show their terroir and vintage."

Farming for Eric was about taste, expression, and health. Hard choices had to be made. Petrochemicals and the carbon footprint are not the only environmental considerations for the soil and the planet. The choice to make a natural wine evolves from a point of view, a belief that pervades every food selection. It is always going to be about the lesser of two evils. But the three people I was going to meet in the next few days were absolutely adamant that their farming was going to be as natural as their wine. Period.

The jagged Montserrat mountain range looked like a crazy paper crown. Oriol Illa of Els Jelipins was late. The sun was brutal. I hugged the disappearing shade. This is not a landscape I am attracted to; being fair, I am inclined to the cool green of Galicia. Looking at the bleached vista, I could have sworn I saw Luis Buñuel's eponymous character of *Viridiana*: the gorgeous, holy, and blonde babe burdened by a heavy wooden cross as she walks for piety.

Buñuel, the exiled filmmaker, made *Viridiana* when Franco invited him back home, promising the auteur complete cinematic freedom. Buried not so subtly in the story was Buñuel's anger with the Catholic Church's support of the dictator. The film was ultimately banned yet won the Palme d'Or. Applicable to the film's subversiveness was a useful and powerful symbol of the fall and resurrection of wine, even natural wine, in Spain.

A truck's rumble rocked me from my hallucinations, and I rolled my bag to the vehicle. "Oriol?" I asked the skinny man with the long fingers of a surgeon and as black-creased as a mechanic's.

It was indeed. Ten minutes later, we arrived at a vineyard that was bordered by olive trees. I had seen that odd-looking collection of vines the other day and had inquired about them as if they were a strange new dog breed.

"Oh, these are yours!" I exclaimed. At times, life was so serendipitous. The vineyard was teensy, just under four acres, and mostly planted to a grape I had no experience with; it was called Sumoll. What struck me about these tall, almost wolfhound-like vines with extremely furry leaves was that they looked as spindly as sumac trees. Their bunches, even at this time in June, when they were green and immature, were long and loose like an elephant's trunk.

"We would hear about Sumoll," Oriol said. "We went to find some and met a grower, very close to La Mata Nova, our home." He was jazzed to find the small plot and set out to rent it and work the land, letting the grape speak for itself.

The Sumoll vines were eighty or so years old. The ground they grew in was spongy from Oriol's care. Filled with slate, basalt, quartz, and sandlike decomposed granite, it was dazzling. Oriol works organically, not biodynamically. "If you work in biodynamics, you work with silica for sun absorption," he said, looking up at the blinding sun. "In Spain, you don't need silica. I work the soil in the winter and then let the weeds just grow. Yes, the weeds compete for water, but we want that." He added sadly, "The DO Penedès doesn't want to encourage Sumoll. They don't think it's grand enough." He caressed a leaf. "But I love it."

We obviously shared the same soft spot for the underdog.

Oriol's story was similar to that of Spain: death and resurrection. At twenty, the young man was miserable, working in a suit and tie in a bank. He tried public relations, yet longed for a more physical existence. As he learned more about wine, he had a growing desire to make it. "One day, I met René Barbier," he said. Barbier is a superstar consultant who works with his wife—another superstar, Sara Perez. "They took me under their wing, because René said, 'You're crazy, like me.'"

Crazy? I looked at the man carefully, dark hair almost painted to his head. Nah, he was merely intense.

He followed them to Priorat, where he met his future wife, Glòria. Together they learned how to make those 92-plus-point wines. Oriol told me that the way they were taught to work—with yeast, new oak, and enzymes—was against everything they believed in. "It was against our nature and I was very unhappy," he said. "I became very disillusioned when I realized that wine, and even celebrated wine, was not poetry, but just a recipe."

"What is the recipe?" I curiously asked.

"Cold soaking up to a week with a ton of sulfur," he said. "Then, inoculate and adjust the temperature to hot—thirty degrees centigrade for fermentation to kick in and to extract all the power out of the grape. Punch down, or pump over, or do both, often."

They also had to give the juice plenty of oxygen—often with a bubbling machine that hyperoxygenates the wine—and then rack it into new barrels and add more oxygen every month. "That's the low-tech version of a recipe wine," Oriol said. "And, by the way, these are also people who consider themselves natural. In 2002, we were going to leave the wine world because it was just too cynical."

Until one day, and there is always that one day, when it changed.

Oriol met the head buyer for Lavinia, the large wine store that originated in Madrid. "She was friends with people in France," he said. "She showed me wines, and I started to see things differently. I started to see what real natural was." That message was driven home when he met Barolo princess, Maria Theresa Mascarello, who told him how a wine could be set free. "We made our first vintage in 2003—without yeast," he said. "My wife was crying every day with fear. We were so afraid because everyone told us the wine wouldn't ferment."

We pulled up to a small café where my friend, the young Spanish wine savior, waited, a cerveza at his fingers. Wearing a baseball cap, eyes hidden behind his Ray-Bans, he held a fat stogie in his fingers. He looked perfect for his role, guarding two men—his West Coast distributor and a New York city salesman named Chris Barnes with dark-ringed eyes and a reptilian, sallow face. I looked at the puddle of canned mussels next to a beer sitting in the middle of the table, and my food-poisoning radar went off. *Poor guy*, I thought.

They had been on the road visiting many of José's producers, including Blomberg, who was having an extremely dramatic spring. The rain! The mold! The rot! He was complaining bitterly; the vintage was going to kill him. Then we took off to Oriol's household, and the road was so twisty I felt as queasy as if I had consumed those tainted tinned mussels.

We alighted at the Els Jelipins world headquarters. Oriol was correct; his home and winery were in the middle of nowhere. His cellar was folded into a tiny room underneath his family's dwelling. Against the emerald-colored wall was an old basket press. "We work dirty," said Oriol, meaning that his equipment is old and the stems are kept on the grapes. "But, we also work clean. To work with little or no sulfur, you must be extremely clean."

This was a message often repeated; little or no sulfur means impeccable hygiene. Also, increasingly, like many others who seek to make a more terroir-influenced wine, Oriol rejects temperature control, cold maceration, pumps, racking, and stainless tanks (he finds the steel gives a lifelessness to wines). Oriol stomps, does the *pigeage* in small barrels, and does not handle the wine once it is in the barrel. This means no *battonage* and no moving the wine before bottling. Of course, Oriol's production is extremely small, so moving everything by hand for a few hundred cases is not like dealing with a production of several thousand. The wine is very expensive, weighing in at about seventy-five dollars a bottle, if you could find it.

Against the wall were two slender amphorae (*ánforas* in Spanish). These ceramic vessels were made in an area of Spain close to the Portuguese border. I had tasted a few wines that were made or raised in them, but I'd never been this close to one.

Josko Gravner, in the Friuli region of northern Italy, is often cited as an inspiration. He brought in the new era of the amphora when he experimented with large Georgian vessels in 1997. Before that, they were pretty much unheard-of and seemed a wacky, even attention-grabbing choice, though they were still traditional in the hinterlands of Soviet Georgia, Turkey, and Extremadura. Gravner had previously bitten hard into new oak barrels, but then embraced amphorae instead, for both fermentation and *élevage*. Increasingly, he left all additives behind, save for some sulfur. By 2001, Gravner was convinced that the 1,500- to 2,000-liter vessel was the one of choice. *The World of Fine Wine* recorded that his stated reason was to return the wine to the soil, which struck me as biblical. Others followed, with different approaches. In Trentino, Elisabetta Foradori does gorgeous work with these vessels for fermentation and some aging. In Sicily on Mt. Etna, the outspoken Frank Cornelissen, like Oriol, prefers using amphorae only for the raising of the wine, not for fermentation. The clay vessels need curing on the inside, but both Foradori and Cornelissen shun the beeswax used by both Oriol and Gravner. Cornelissen says that if he could afford it, porcelain would be the perfect sealant. He's looking for a vessel that gives absolutely no flavor to the wine.

Wine needs what the French call *élevage*, raising up. The vessel choice for that period of maturation is one way in which the winemaker has personal expression, which I see as a matter of voice, as opposed to manipulation. Here is one of the places where the hand of man appears in the taste of the wine. Oriol wants to express an "ancient" wine, as does Gravner. Cornelissen, the pragmatist, just wants to make a modern wine that is the most transparent translation of terroir he can manage.

I knew that Foradori had told me that she loved her new amphorae because she saw that her wines found their identity in them quicker. But wondering what Oriol would say, I asked, "But couldn't you get the same result from a cement tank instead of an ánfora?"

"Ánfora," he said, "is a very interesting wine recipient for its characteristics: soft, ambient temperature variation. The shape naturally puts the wine in movement, so the lees move around naturally. It is clean and you can change its porosity." He then said his wife was waiting for lunch.

Glòria Garriga is one of those slender beauties who bakes bread, has an extensive herbal garden, and built her house around a cactus rather than remove it. She stewed up a traditional chickpea dish. Watching all the men, save Chris, who just couldn't eat, heap their plates, and having just heard Miguel Torres tell me how he loves nothing better than chickpeas, I became convinced that these humble beans should be added to the list of culinary aphrodisiacs. Even if there's lamb on the table, it is the chickpea that wins.

Throughout the meal, we tasted the various vintages of the wines. Sumoll turned out to be tannic, somewhere between Barolo and Sagrantino. The vintages were wildly different, but always present in both was an appealing, bitter tannin. José kept on saying, "Oh wow," which seemed perfectly articulate for a wine that surprises.

The 2003 was almost bricklike, with lots of Indian spices such as cumin and turmeric, balanced out by white fruit like a white gooseberry, and dried cherry with Earl Grey tea. "The human hand cannot be removed from terroir, the intention and the spirit," Oriol said and then continued, telling us what he wanted to create. "When you drink a wine and you feel impressed and can't describe it, that's what I want."

I understood what he meant. I recently viewed a promotional video by James Suckling, who had been a critic with the *Wine Spectator* for many years. In the film clip, he is manically grading wine by points. Over and over again, he numerically rates the wines: "I give this ninety-seven points. I give this a hundred points. That is perfect. A perfect wine. One hundred points." The idea of a perfect wine is an insane aspiration. I could imagine a wine being perfect in a moment, as in a moment of perfect bliss, but if a wine is natural, it will taste somewhat differently every time you taste it. Sometimes it will show off; sometimes it will be shy. Natural wines can be as moody as I am. But a perfect number for a wine, I find insulting. Oriol sought an ideal in wine, an unbearable lightness of being captured in the wine, for which there could be no numeric.

He just might have succeeded: Months later, I poured the 2004 Els Jelipins at an Austin, Texas, wine dinner. As if on cue, people who didn't know each other put their nose in their glass, and all of the sudden, just what José had now expressed was echoed around the table: "Oh wow." That is the inarticulate reaction of straightforward shock and delight. It was exactly the kind of wine Oriol wanted to make. It is not scorable; it just . . . is.

Our tasting at Glòria and Oriol's table now dissolved into talk, and José, quite comfortable at the head of the table, asked, "Alice, how was that Eco conference?"

I told him and the others at the table about the transgenic potato and something else. "The most curious thing happened at the Q and A. A gentleman in the second row raised his hand. He was older, baldish, and proper. Turns out he said he was writing a wine guide and wanted to know why organic and biodynamic wines are not as good as the conventional wines. From the sound of the question, I took him for an amateur, so I took the approach that I'd have to see what he was tasting and what his palate was like. I had the feeling he had a very different one from mine. I then tried to explain terroir to him and how those of us who like natural wines often find it the best way to express terroir, but not all terroir has something to say. Turns out he was . . . Peñín of the Peñín Wine Guide!"

They all started to laugh. José's eyes almost bugged out of his head. "You're kidding me," he said. It did seem inconceivable that one of the most prominent figures of Spanish wine criticism was dismissive of a category that inspires. (In the fall of 2010, José Peñín became interested in natural wine and went to visit Laureano Serres in Terra Alta and bought several bottles to take home.)

After we helped Chris stuff his pocket with sage and mint to help ease his stomach, we left for our next stop, Jordi Sanfeliu's vineyard, a new José discovery. We climbed into José's vehicle, slamming the heavy doors and racing the clock against nightfall. In short order, we begged him to please kill his techno club music. Settled into the more sensual saxophone of Lester Young, we were delayed often by having to stop for our sick passenger. By the time we reached DO Costers del Segre after a harrowing ride, I crawled out of José's vinomobile, gasping for the fresh, unpolluted air, quite carsick myself. Those twisty roads of Spain are sometimes just too much. Note to self—drive. Always.

Jordi rushed out to greet us. He was dressed in a very definite worker blue. His hair was oiled from work sweat, yet silky. His eyes were blue ice, his manner warm. He embraced José more like a younger brother than a new importer.

"You go ahead," Chris said to us, barely opening his eyes. He was going to miss something amazing, but when you succumb to food poisoning from eating a sick mussel, what else can you do? We left him to sleep it off.

Jordi's family had been farmers for generations. His parents still work in the vines. We passed their ancient olive trees, lentils in flower, and the almonds that were waiting for fruit and reached his vines, which in mid-June were still not parched by summer's heat and were among the most beautiful I'd ever seen. Growing without any help were volunteer wild leeks, asparagus, poppies, and carrots. The grasses were silky, fragile, and kiwi green, never touched by chemicals. Until he made wine—his first vintage in 2005—Jordi was selling his grapes. He sold them to the likes of the huge Cava producer, Freixenet. I felt like crawling up under the vines in the early evening sky and falling asleep in those pastoral vineyards. This was far from the harshness of a Buñuel-like landscape, of green bushes springing from tan and parched soil.

"People farm with chemicals; it's a drug," Jordi said. José seemed stunned into stupefaction by the area's beauty. In a jolt, he snapped out of it and began to pop off photos of the poppy-flecked vines, capturing the huge shards—slabs, really—of limestone.

We had entered a world of waking dreams and soon ended up in a cherry orchard right next to the vines, and we greedily started to stuff our faces and gather cherries in our shirts for dinner. Every tree had a different taste, a different-sized fruit. The night was at that magic moment when you could feel the seconds turning into darkness. But Jordi had something else to show us. In the middle of the tree was a big white box. Jordi knelt down and flipped a switch. Music! Flashing strobe! "Deesco!" he shouted.

We were doubled over. Tears ran down our cheeks. José was giggling like a maniac. "It feels good to laugh," he managed to say, a favorite phrase of his. We were all holding our *estómagos* because we were going at it so hard. Jordi's low-tech desperation act against the attack of wild boars was priceless. "They run away. No neighbors around to complain." What a brain that Jordi had.

At midnight, we followed Jordi to a one-row town, just over the border in Tarragona, with ten dogs and forty cats. We had an entire five-floor house to ourselves. Dinner waited, prepared by friends of his. We were like little kids in summer camp. There was prep to be done. Chris hit the couch, and the rest of us got to work cooking, chopping, and popping open bottles. It was near two in the morning when we sat down at the table. José had brought an entire case of wines he wanted to taste from his travels, hoping to make a discovery. José kept on opening the wines from his travel stash, and we kept on pouring them out, until we gave up. Unfortunately, they were all terribly sulfured, and after drinking Jordi's rosé made from the Trépat grape, we found it just difficult to go back to normal wine. We surrendered to the Trépat. The wine was like crack; it was all we wanted. "You know, Alice, this is so delicious, it's like La Signora's."

José and I would always have La Signora.

We drank until 4 A.M. and then teetered to bed. And the (sometimes) miracle of no-sulfur wine? There were no hangovers.

Another morning turned into another chunk of paradise. Our leader pronounced, "We're staying here."

"What about Laureano?" I asked. Ever since I had seen him at La Remise, the madman of the town of Pinell de Brai was the main reason for my journey to the wilds of Terre Alta. Hooking up with José and the boys, and the idyll into Tarragona, was a bonus.

"Chris is still not feeling well," José explained, and he was right. The boy was still green around the gills. I had been hijacked from my original plan. Not unwillingly, I might add. Jordi and his wines were worth the detour, and thanks to Chris, we had another day in paradise, a gift. We had that one extra day of bliss. Plus, I had wireless. Who could be happier?

Usually a workaholic, I gave myself over to the day, to play and to enjoy the attention of five fantastic men. I contributed a roasted cauliflower to the array of grilled sausages, salads. The day was clear; the olive trees were our audience. We idled in the sun, drinking rosé.

In the heat of the late afternoon, sated from their lamb, the boys went to nap while I helped Jordi clean up. He knew no English, I knew no Catalan, so we gave French a shot, and miraculously, it worked.

Why does a farm boy with little exposure to the outside world think to make wine without sulfur? Turns out the transformation was simple, as it was for Todd Blomberg. Jordi started producing organic olive oil because he didn't want to pollute the soil or the body. Similarly, he had this notion of a pure wine with nothing added. "But technology is good," he said. "This is why I thank the Internet, so I could research some background and found Laureano."

Yes, Laureano Serres. I feared he was twiddling his thumbs waiting for his guests.

The dishes were cleaned. The boys started to surface from their naps with bags packed. Chris finally looked truly better. We knew we could thank the Trépat for his new health, and we left our paradise somewhere around six o'clock. With the others in the back of the vehicle for another nap, I gabbed in the front with José. I adored José.

I don't use that word lightly. While he was far from innocent—he left home at an early age—he had an innocence about the wine. His love for the growers was infectious. Since we initially met, he had been revamping his portfolio. In one short year, he had weeded out the wines that were "espoofulated." Even bolder was his move to stop showing his wines to *The Wine Advocate*. When José and I first met, he was presenting his wines for review in this influential wine publication, which is famous for popularizing the notion of grading a wine on the hundred-point scale. But when he fine-tuned his collection of winemakers to the more natural-minded, he stopped staging special tastings for their critique. "My wines aren't for them," he explained. "I like Jay Miller [the Spanish wine reviewer for *The Wine Advocate*] a lot. He's a sweet guy. But really, these wines shouldn't be sold by a number. I see how awarding points to wine destroyed Spain. People started to make wines to those points and then used tricks to make them taste in a way so the reviewers would like them. I don't want to be part of that system."

I have to respect the man for having the courage to say no to the power nexus. After all, the owner of *The Wine Advocate*, Robert M. Parker Jr., is a very powerful man in the world of wine and in the world of selling wines. The piece that I wanted to know is how José had his consciousness changed.

"How did you decide you wanted to bring in wines that are more natural?" I asked. "How did you even know they existed?"

I shouldn't have been surprised by the answer. "In 2007, I had a Marcel Lapierre unsulfured wine," he said. "I had never had anything as pure as that. It was like drinking water from heaven."

We were back to Marcel.

Finally, we approached Pinell de Brai. Laureano was waiting in the doorway of his house and winery, swearing he didn't mind that we were three-quarters of a day late; it allowed him to go to his niece's confirmation. Yet still, we felt guilty, or at least I did.

Where Jordi's energy was more like the sparkle in a cava, Laureano was a forceful gush of fermentation. I could only imagine what it would be like to be married to this artistic, ADD-riddled genius who used only rainwater to clean his equipment. Sweet torture. Thankfully, it's his wife—and not me—who gets to be either long-suffering or constantly amused by Laureano. One thing is for sure: Like his wines, Laureano is without artifice.

Again, we were on a mad rush to reach the vines before sunset. Happily, in under five minutes, we were standing among the little globes of Laureano's Macabeo vines. It was such a gorgeous sunset, we were almost speechless for a while, talking this and that, history, hows, whys, looking at his soil, looking at the vines.

"You can't treat a plant like a human being but you have to respect each one," Laureano said, turning to one of his vines, bending down as if he was addressing it. "So I ask them, What do you want? Harvest? And I have to listen. If they say, Pick me, everything else in winemaking is automatic."

These Catalonians certainly step up to their charmingly mad reputation.

The night was magnificent. The giant lantern of Jupiter hung low in the midnight blue sky, striated with blonde sunset highlights in the darkened west. With the boys talking and laughing in the background, and José polluting the fresh air with a cigar, I thought about what made someone like Todd a Todd, and Jordi a Jordi, and Laureano a Laureano? What was their motivation—to suffer, to be poor even?

Since 2010, the category of natural wine became a phenomenon both inside and out of the hipster world. Williamsburg in Brooklyn was crawling with wine lists devoted to natural wines; a store opened up with a dedication to them as well. The London scene has conflagrated, initially sparked mostly by the famous unconventional wine bar, Terroirs Wine Bar & Restaurant in the very conventional Trafalgar Square. Tokyo was the first to hook on to the wines, attracted by the purity, but now, the thirst has even spread to Hong Kong. This Chinese city is mostly famous for its thirst for Bordeaux, as 2010 saw Hong Kong's first natural-wine bar. Yet, the more the wines became sought out, the more the naysayers inevitably showed up on bulletin boards and in articles, writing that the term *natural* was a slogan. Natural, they said, was only a marketing tool.

The biggest nose-thumbing came from Robert Parker in 2010: "About these 'natural,' unmanipulated and pure wines: One of the major scams being foisted on wine consumers is the so-called 'natural' wine movement" (*Wine Advocate*, issue 191).

Parker is still the most powerful voice in the business, and it is difficult to see what his motivation could be for this slur. Natural wines could be considered anti-points wines. Was his establishment (and *Wine Spectator*'s as well), which is based on points, threatened? I do believe in Parker's sincerity, so what I really began to suspect was whether his fame kept him sequestered. Did he spend so little time (or no time) in the vineyards with people making wine—people living their lives so close to nature—that he just failed to see—no pun intended—the point?

The people who choose to make wine in this way have a compelling single-mindedness. In an interview about her latest novel, Cynthia Ozick spoke to the *New York Times* about passion: "Is there a word more passionate than passion? Obsession, total immersion, the feeling that everything else doesn't matter."

Her words describe these men and women of the vine. What compels me to write about them is not the size of the domaine. It isn't about small and cute and photogenic; it is about the intensity, passion, and commitment—and, of course, the tastes. Other people get a charge from extreme sports. I get it from extreme winemaking and its people.

Laureano loaded up the car with bottles. He was determined to make us taste every little cuvée he ever made. We arrived at our next house rental, where 120 euros got us much smaller and less refined lodging. We were no longer in paradise. The stove didn't work. We couldn't find a corkscrew. We tried to create a rustic meal with the provisions we brought from town and the dull knife that the landlord had provided us with. Laureano started to open up the bottle with his shoe, taking out the last bit of cork with his teeth. The shoe trick was something that some wine people have learned in case of a wine emergency. Having seen it on YouTube, I thought it was only a joke; after all, the trick is quite brutal to the wine. Seeing it in the flesh had us rolling on the floor, breathless and pained with laughter.

Thankfully, we soon finally found a corkscrew, or Laureano would have needed a dentist. Tasting with him was a roller-coaster ride. He excels in wines made in an oxidative manner. Most of the world tries to keep wine away from oxygen, as it starts to degrade and lose freshness. But when the barrels aren't topped off and the wine starts to evaporate, a layer of yeast called flor develops on the top and is responsible for the unusual taste of Sherry as well as for many of the wines in the Jura. The wines then evolve to a more earth and nut profile, and with the acidity, which can zing, what emerges is a profoundly different and electric kind of wine.

I once had a British journalist by the name of Stuart George over for dinner with a few individuals who shared my palate. As it happened, three of the white wines we drank that night were made under a flor. One of the wines was a sulfured Savagnin from the Jura. The other was Laureano's Yes! It is a fabulous oxidative white wine (well, orange, really, as it was made with some extended skin contact, giving the white wine a faint orange tinge) from those Macabeu grapes. No sulfur at all. The writer, an amiable fellow, has won awards for wine writing, documented this evening and his wine experience in *Langton's* Magazine:

> The use of sulphur with natural wines is contentious. In principle, a bare minimum is used but the bravest (some would say most foolish) winemakers don't use any at all, which makes the wine highly prone to oxidation and microbial growth. Wines like this are unlikely to travel well, as Alice's tasting proved. The priestess's and the congregation's wines were invariably oxidised and had acidity like a banshee's wail, more suggestive of unripe grapes than cool climate viticulture. Natural as they were, I took no pleasure in drinking them. I like freshness and balance, not decay and a kick in the face. I think of these wines as I do of Vegemite and Aussie Rules—I like the idea more than the reality.

Like many other journalists who view knocking natural wines as sport, this writer made the mistake of believing oxidation is the mark of a natural wine, forgetting entirely that the Jura white we had tasted was actually not a natural wine at all. Not only that, but the grapes in the bottles were plenty ripe. This was not the problem. The only problem was his lack of experience with them. Cutting him some slack, I'm not aware of how many of these wines are available for him to experience in his home country. There's no doubt that some drinkers have a hard time with the odd taste of nut instead of fruit. He can say that these wines are not his cup of tea. He should, however, not mistake this style of wine as a hallmark of *vin naturel*.

Not all natural wines are delicious. Like other wines, there are the good, the bad, and the indifferent. However, I will dare to say that those of us who love natural do indeed have a greater tolerance (as well as thirst) for more irregularity and for different styles of wine within the category: orange, wispy, concentrated, and, yes, oxidative.

When I asked Laureano why he chose to make wines in this oxidative way, he answered, "There has always been a tradition of these wines here in Terre Alta." He was determined to keep the tradition alive.

Laureano used to make wine conventionally. For three years, he vinified with sulfur, but he was unhappy, "I don't like sulfur. You add it to a wine, and it changes. First you have a live color . . . then it's not live anymore. You make sulfur; the color is dead." He said that wine has the ability to bounce back from the dead after it is sulfured. "But at the beginning, it goes, *ouaaa!*" He flung his arms out from his body, as if he were a bat scooping up the mosquitoes. "But the wine comes back. Yes. The wine comes back. But I don't like. One day, I read an article that said it was possible to make wine without sulfur. This was 2004, without knowing anyone in France, just with Internet, I find."

Laureano experimented. Benoit, the man who runs Anima de Vi, a wine store in Barcelona, heard about him and went to Pinell to visit. "Benoit comes and says, 'You work without sulfur, but do you know in France there's a movement?' He put me in touch with Thierry Puzelat. *Ouaaa!* He told me I have to go to Remise. This was December 2005. I go there, and I drink and then I drive home after the wines? No trouble. After I go to Auvergne and to the Jura. I go to Overnoy. I go with a full car. With me are Giles Azonni, Axel Pruffer. Pfifferling. Frenchie! *Ouaaa! Ouaaa! Ouaaa! Ouaaa!* Overnoy! *Ouaaa!* We go to Overnoy for a meeting. Overnoy! He makes bread. He makes bread! And I like bread. I love bread. He takes me to crack nuts and eat bread. Pierre Overnoy. This is my first moment. It's good. Sometimes, I see a respect that is not deserved. But Overnoy? *Ouaaa!*"

There was hero worship in his story, and I shared his hero worship of Pierre Overnoy, whom I had the chance to visit, to taste the bread, to drink his Ploussard and his Savagnin and his Chardonnay. On my first visit to his home, he pedantically instructed, "A taste is like a wave. You must capture the first sniff and watch the evolution. Look not for the wine's length, but for how pretty it is." If there ever was a genuine man, Pierre Overnoy was he. Marketing scam? Indeed.

These were the gods of natural winemaking for Laureano, and each of them went back to Chauvet and Néauport. Laureano created the Productores de Vinos Naturales organization in Spain. There were others. I kept on thinking of what Henry Miller said about Luis Buñuel: "Traitor, anarchist, pervert, defamer, iconoclast. But lunatic they do not call him."

This was applicable to all of the Spanish wine renegades.

I was in bed before Laureano drove home at 5:30 in the morning. Every once in a while I heard José break out in a laugh and Laureano shouting, "Ouaaa!" We left the house a mess. Though it was not a rock-star trashing of the place, it was—trust me—a mess.

CHAPTER 8

Chauvetists or Néauportists?

Science is organized knowledge. Wisdom is organized life.

—IMMANUEL KANT

Ever since that afternoon in Valvigneres, the name Jacques Néauport kept resurfacing with increasing frequency. It was at the wine bar Le Verre Volé that Jean-Paul Rocher had told me unequivocally to go and see him. A filmmaker in the Loire wrote to me about this fabulous fellow he met, quite agreeable but shy—Jacques Néauport. But when a random e-mail came my way from an itinerant biodynamic student staying in Santa Rosa, telling me that he had decided that Jacques Néauport was going to be my husband, I had to do something proactive. First, however, I declined his matchmaking offer. Sixty-three and living with a mother in a remote town in the hills was not my type. Still, if I needed to find the origin of the natural-wine movement, I had no choice but to return to the Ardèche. Néauport was the most direct living link.

Everyone was on board to help me make contact. Andrea Calek sent me Jacques's phone number and address, delivering the ultimate blow: "No e-mail." Worried about how my French would perform over the phone, I asked Pascaline to give him a call. At precisely 10 A.M. on the next morning, she called me back. I could hear her grinning as she delivered the news. "It would be his pleasure," she reported. "By the way, he speaks perfect English, and he invites you to lunch."

This was too easy. Where was the resistance? I thought I'd have to bring on the heroics. For some reason, I had expected him to hang up on Pascaline. I expected I would need Andrea to plead my case. Yes, someone had called him a "charming fellow" and an unsung saint, but I had heard so many other descriptions of him— reclusive, paranoid, difficult.

The lunch invitation made me feel uncomfortable. I conduct interviews more efficiently when I'm hungry. Then there was the meat issue. "His mother," I said to Pascaline, "will be cooking for days. I can't show up and then tell her I don't eat animal." When company comes, the vegetables go out the window and the duck confit flies in.

Trying to stave off an elderly woman's horror as I sat at her table pushing the food around on my plate, I took on an archaic task I wrote a letter on paper. I jotted down that I was coming, and delighted. Would the twenty-ninth of September be okay? I hated to be a bother, but I felt it was best to advise his mother that one of her American guests, me, was a pain in the ass. I had Amy Lillard call to make sure the letter was received. "He was lovely!" she reported. I bought a plane ticket to head to France for the most expensive lunch I'd ever planned.

Although I didn't know Amy very well, I had presumed on her hospitality on three separate occasions in eight months. I had seen her vines in their winter slumber and at first flower, and now, I'd be there when the grapes were busy turning sugar into alcohol. Toward the end of September 2010, I arrived at the Avignon train station, once again waiting for Amy to pick me up.

Back at her place in St. Quentin la Poterie, we tasted through the slightly warm and fizzy 2010. It was only a few days old and still sweet. "Some fierce tannins in there," I noted. When I retired, I prudently checked my bed for scorpions. I was grateful to see none. However, to remind me that an idyll like Peter Mayle's *Year in Provence* was not for me, there hugging the wall in the bathroom was a huge spider, looking like an anemic tarantula. "Matt!" I screamed out to Amy's husband.

In the morning before we left, Amy did her rustic pump-overs and punch-downs on her wines, and we took to the road. Before we left, I insisted that she bring one of her wines. "You know he's going to ask," I said.

She demurred. "Aw, I don't want to! It's not their thing."

I reminded her how sad she was in the end that she hadn't brought some with her on our Valvigneres adventure. Emboldened, she grabbed a 2008. We keyed in "Saint-Fortunat sur Eyrieux" into her GPS and hit the road. For two hours, we traced the twirl of the Rhône river north, heading west into the hills, into the overgrowth of the Ardèche, into purity, part the Swiss alpine foothills' mintiness. We reached the destination and parked in front of a café with no customers.

The town was home to the expected feral cats. "There is no irony in rural France," was Amy's commentary as we passed dwellings bedecked with gnomes and fairies. We soon came to the end of the village, and there on that street was a narrow house cheerily decorated with geraniums and wine bottles on the steps' landing, guarding a screen door. At the base of the stairs was a sign: Néauport.

That's when I turned mentally clammy. "I always get so nervous before an interview," I said. "But what if I came all this way for nothing?"

Amy tried to help me focus. "What do you want out of this?" she asked. "Why did you come all the way here?"

Because I'm a fool, I berated myself. Like a character in a play, I wanted to make sure something was learned at the end. Arriving on the man's doorstep was a little late in the game for me to be deeply pondering that question. Yet I walked away from his doorway and started to think out loud. "Néauport knew Chauvet better than any person alive today. This is the place to come to find out the truth about that cold carbonic method."

Amy's blonde head nodded in encouragement as she asked, "And?"

"But, Amy, if I go at him like that—if I ask him, 'So, Jacques, you know all of those wines that are marked first by carbonic maceration and mask terroir—do we have you to thank?' he'll throw me out, and I wouldn't blame him. But, how do I pose this: 'Jules only advocated carbonic maceration for Gamay on granite, yet you helped people all over the country on all sorts of soils to make wine in this method. In fact, Jacques, for better or worse, you have promoted the aromas and flavors of this technique that, right or wrong, have become synonymous with natural wine. And isn't it true that people like Christian Chaussard in the Loire are moving away from the method and wanting to discover real terroir, going back to a traditional fermentation? And anyway, what is so natural about filling a tank with carbon dioxide or dry ice?' All of that is irrelevant, because the real reason I spent a thousand dollars on Air France is to find out from the source how this trend toward making wine with little else but grapes started. And you know what? I just want to see what Néauport is like. How lame is that?"

"It will be fine," Amy said reassuringly.

I knew I was relying on her to be charming if I messed up.

We returned and walked up the steps. On the landing, I could see that those bottles were older vintages of Lapierre, Overnoy, and Maupertuis. It was then that it registered: He had acted as a consultant to them all. "What a wine cellar," I remarked. Even though it was only noon, I was thirsty.

"I bet these bottles are for lunch," said Amy as she prepared to knock.

"If only we could be so lucky," I said, forever the optimist. With that, the door was creaked opened by a bespectacled man with a tense but very friendly smile. He had a winsome head of brilliant white hair as well as a sparse white growth sprouting up, walrus-like, from his neck. Of middle height and slender build, he was dressed for spring on that fall day. He sported a nautical theme: white pants, striped sailor shirt. I had been expecting someone tall and rotund. He shook my hand, pumping it enthusiastically. Yes, it was Jacques.

"Come in!" he said.

Earthy smells from roasted olives, eggplant, and potted meats drew us into the kitchen, where another part of the scene startled me. There, squished around the kitchen table, Jacques's eighty-eight-year-old mother, Ginette, hovered over a small crowd of people.

In addition to Amy, Jacques, and me, there were Ginette; her somewhat older sister, Henriette; Jacques's cousin; her husband, "from the north" (whatever that meant); a winemaker; and his girl-friend, who also happened to be Jacques's new publisher (one of those gorgeous, thin, tall beauties who smoke and have a beautiful name—Isabelle). Jacques had turned our intense tête-à-tête into a party. I thought to myself, *This is not what I had in mind for a quiet interview.*

The kitchen was washed in pales, the chairs were rickety, and the tablecloth was waxed. Who could see it, anyway, as the table was piled with olives, glasses, and that mouthwateringly red Provençal pizza called *pissaladière*. A crusty, dense medieval bread commanded the table and seemed large enough to feed a small village for a week. A globe of cabbage poked out from the sink, and Ginette, a country cook with a floury face, happily fussed over her guests, whom she was prepared to stuff, as if she had planned to extract our foies at the end.

Jacques had planned an icebreaker game for us: Which Clairette de Die was better? The local bubbly wine was poured. We toasted, making direct eye contact with each person about to sip, as one does in Europe. Then, with a nervous rush of energy, Jacques commanded, "Prenez-vous vos verres, et rendons-nous à la terrace." Leaving his mother and aunt behind in the kitchen, we, the seven others, headed to the terrace, or rather, the tiny landing where those wine bottles stood upright. I knew what was coming, be-cause in the rolling foothills of his bucolic village of Pupillin, Pierre Overnoy had already inducted me into this tasting ritual. Shortly after entering his home, Pierre handed me a glass and then guided me outside into his back garden. As if he were talking about the pope, he said, "Monsieur Chauvet always believed that one needs to taste in the fresh air." He and I stood in the pure Pupillin breezes, our noses in our glasses. I waited for his cue, for him to take the first sip, and then I followed.

This was exactly what Jacques had in mind, an homage to Chauvet. This technique really does affect the perception of aroma and taste, but I'm not sure it's as effective on my New York City rooftop as it was on Jacques's sweet landing in Saint-Fortunat. After the frenzied sniff, we soon returned for more hors d'oeuvres and conversation in the kitchen, putting quite the dent into the olives, bread, and pizza. Sitting next to one another, Jacques and I slowly made our way into preliminary conversation. He announced to me that in his study down the hallway were twenty years of his personal tasting notes. The house was petite. He didn't have a computer. There must have been files rat-packing the room that already had little space for a desk and chair. With this Dickensian vision in my mind, I was surprised when he, the man without computer, went into that office and emerged with a huge digital camera around his neck, a nod to modernity. Contradictions exist everywhere.

Then he leaned into me and said, "I hear Marcel is at the end."

This was so disturbing, though not entirely unexpected. Jacques hadn't actually seen Marcel since 1996, when he had left the Beaujolais. Those years were formative ones for both of them, historic ones for the wine world. I hoped the news about Marcel was just wrong gossip. Yet, I knew it was probably true. When I had been with Marcel, I had the feeling that he looked at his vineyards as if it might be his last vintage. There was that careful quality to the way his wife and son addressed him at lunch. During the summer, his annual party had been staged on an earlier date, and it was the biggest ever, as if everyone came to say good-bye. For someone who had once been very close to Marcel, Jacques delivered the news with detachment and then became an easy interviewee. So easy, he anticipated questions before they came out of my mouth.

"I met Chauvet in 1977," he started. Seems that Jacques took a painter friend of his to attend a lecture Chauvet was giving about making wine without sulfur. "I had read some of Chauvet's scientific writings and wanted to meet him. But when I heard him talk, I thought he was absolutely insane. I almost didn't want to believe," Jacques told me. "I went over to talk to him with a friend. We were not very polite. Yet Chauvet was very nice and invited us to visit. My friend said, 'I'm not going to visit that stupid old man.' But I did. I was intrigued, in fact. I liked him. I went to visit with him and then immediately started to work for him. I realized how much better my own wine could have been if I had met Chauvet earlier. Better barrels, better grape, quicker into the bottle."

Put into context, the late 1970s was an era for searching. The year 1977 was ten years after Woodstock and two after the end of the Vietnam War. It was also the year that Elvis died; Bob Dylan's first wife, Sarah, filed for divorce; and *Saturday Night Fever* celebrated disco. Shunning the popular music of the day, I retreated into the safety of blues, jazz, folk, and classical. I escaped the trashy 1970s fashions by wearing vintage and Indian imports. I experimented with German wines, which were plentiful, cheap, and better than Mateus yet high on the sulfur. I didn't even know Loire made wine. I didn't know there was a village that mattered called Morgon.

"But why were you interested in making wine without sulfur in the first place?" I asked.

Jacques started to laugh. It took him a while to speak. "Because we were drunkards!" he finally blurted out.

I'd come to the oracle for the answer, and all he had for me was a punch line. I had no doubt he'd been stumbling drunk plenty of times. His crowd loved to drink, and he wanted to reduce the potential day-after headaches. Sure. I understood this. But the difference between being a drunk and loving to drink is huge. I do the latter and rarely am the former. It was amusing to imagine an entire international movement igniting solely to escape a hangover, but I felt that Jacques was doing himself and the community a disservice insisting that mere hangover avoidance was their main motivation.

Of course, I had heard the explanation before. Dard & Ribo gave it as their main incentive for making their sulfur-free wines, and it was also cited for the Nuits d'Ivresse cuvée made by Catherine and Pierre Breton. But except for some cuvées, both winemakers have moved away from the cold carbonic method of fermentation, which had become associated with *vins de soif*, one face of the natural-wine genre. *Vins de soif* are thirst quenchers, and some of us feel that they leave terroir behind.

There is a place for both kinds of wines—easy-drinking and terroir based—but Jacques didn't seem to be concerned with a wine's longevity or varietal trueness or faithfulness to place. It wouldn't have been the first time that two different aspirations reached the same conclusion. After all, for some people, a hallucinogen gives a mystical experience; for others, it's a party drug.

What was even more curious to me was how Jacques didn't see the connection to Guy Debord. Back when Jacques was a dark-haired man, he hung out with artists, sculptors, and other creative sorts who socialized around wine. One of his friends, the writer-philosopher Alain Braik, was friends with philosopher Debord.

I indulged myself in imagining the conversations, the fights, the banter, the bottles drained well into the wee hours. I envisioned scenes out of D. H. Lawrence, the brotherhood of men drinking and fighting naked in front of the fireplace.

Jacques made fun of my romantic musings. "Alice, there was no direct link between *vin naturel* and philosophy," he said. "The only link is that Alain and Guy used to be incredibly heavy drinkers. Charles Bukowski was a monk compared to them. Alain and Guy found that drinking sans soufre *meant they didn't have hangovers.*"

Yet, the wines must have spoken to Debord on a whole other level. In 1989, Debord's *Panegyric* was published. In this book, he asserted that the majority of wines had lost their authenticity, because of the world market and industrial production. He said they might have labels that look familiar, but what was inside the bottles was undrinkable.

Debord wrote *Panegyric* in late stages of his alcoholism. Earlier on, though, in 1973, when the thinker was more idealistic and healthier in his body, he wrote *Society of the Spectacle*. The earlier book suggested that the development of modern society in the authentic social life had been replaced with its representation: "All that was once directly lived had become mere representation." Such ideas could have been the treatise for the natural-wine movement.

And so the connection to Guy Debord is not such a stretch. After all, Marcel had told of the post–World War II recipe for Beaujolais, which involved those very unripe grapes that needed major reconfiguration and adulteration to become wine.

Over the years, as more technology became available, the recipe for wine was fine-tuned. What emerged was a modern-day, New World–like version of Audibert's *L'art de faire les vins d'imitation,* even for what is considered fine wine. Much of today's wine starts with picking grapes at their maximum ripeness, often when the fruit is out of balance. Then, sulfur is added to kill everything off. The grapes are inoculated and then fermented with enzymes and other products for desired color, texture, flavor, and acidity and are often subject to processes and machines to fine-tune it all, including the amount of alcohol. The result, be it in Audibert's days, Marcel's early history, or right now, is not wines but representations of wines.

When natural wine fought back against the false, it reclaimed its farm-to-table directness; it delivered wine without artifice. With so many highly processed brands lining the wine store shelves, it's no wonder that in their adulterated wake are drinkers and winemakers looking for naked, unadorned, and true.

"Debord was France's most important philosopher," stated Jacques. I wondered if his pride lay in the fact that Debord had drunk many wines, probably exclusively, that he, Jacques, had consulted on. Anyway, *sans soufre* didn't save Debord. He died of alcoholism. Or rather, in 1994, he took control and put a bullet in his heart before his liver could give out. *Sans soufre* or not, alcohol in excess is dangerous for more reasons than just the sulfur.

The others at the table were having a great time. With the growing noise level, we kept on losing the thread of our conversation. Jacques motioned that we should leave the fray and head outside to talk in peace. A mist was falling. The weather in those quiet hills was changeable. Jacques had something to say to me—something important. I waited. I listened.

"I know you are looking for answers, but I have none. There is no recipe," he said, apologetically.

This no-recipe chorus was becoming a theme. Ever suspicious, I dug a little more. "Could you tell me why, if Chauvet didn't use

carbonic in his last vintages, and if Chauvet was the father of natural, why does the method still persist as 'Méthode Chauvet?'"

Then he surprised me, not because of what he said, but because
he said it. "Carbonic is not the only way, Alice, just one. You see,
inside the vintage, there is no dogma. When you work without
sulfur, you must work very carefully, very cleanly, and work with
nature. If you change your regions, you must adapt your ways of
working. You have to notice everything. You cannot adapt if you
follow a recipe."

I had thought I was so damned clever the night that I had
blurted out to Eric that at Ten Bells, the Chauvetists were really
Néauportists. It looked as if I was wrong, at least on the level of
recipe. On the other hand, when it came to the difference of a wine
of terroir or a wine of charm, I might have been correct. There was
that issue with dry ice.

"Jacques, who was it who started to use dry ice in fermentations,
you or Chauvet?"

He started to chuckle. "I had the idea, and Chauvet said, try it.
It was hot, and we went to a neighbor who had a lot of it. We kept
on going back for more, until the neighbor said, enough! But this
kind of cold carbonic has nothing to do with making wine without
sulfur, but prevents the vats from getting dangerously hot."

It also heightened the aromatics.

Jacques's first concern, after all, was aspiring to create a *vin de
soif*, even if terroir was sacrificed. People incorporated the method
but overlooked the process behind it; they followed his lead instead of thinking for themselves. As Marie Lapierre said, "It is dangerous to follow dogma without thinking." Those who just follow
a recipe might be the ones making wines that give some natural
wines a bad name.

"People treated me like a saint," he said, leaning into me. "I went around delivering the gospel." He laughed as if this were a terribly amusing thought. "But that's not for me. It is not my character. What I am proud of is that everyone I worked with went on to be great."

In front of me, standing in the Ardèche freshness, was the Michel Rolland of the natural set. The difference is that the famed flying wine maker (the Bordeaux-based Rolland) drove a Bentley and was rich. Jacques never held a driver's license and lived with his mother. He didn't see himself as a Rolland. He saw himself more as a Kerouac. "Kerouac said he would stop writing when he reached a million words, and I promised I would stop helping people when I helped to make one thousand wines."

I had never heard that Kerouac quote, but I rolled with it. "And did you ever make that many?" I asked him.

He giggled again. "I made two thousand wines!"

Said more like a mentor than a consultant. If two thousand wines were true, no wonder unsulfured wines, and perhaps a certain way of making them—that carbonic method—spread through the natural-wine community in all areas of France.

We returned to the kitchen, where the eating and conversation were in high gear. No one seemed to have noticed our absence. Ginette demanded we take ourselves and appetites into the dining room, where confit was waiting. We were stunned, as plenty of food had already been consumed; we needed second stomachs for this second lunch. Jacques was laughing again. The man liked to giggle. "Three people called to warn me that you didn't eat meat," he said. "They also told me you liked mushrooms and eggs." He walked me over to the rear French doors, where on the little sill was a basket of the most gorgeous golden fat fans of chanterelles. "I picked them," he said.

The special attention was embarrassing, yet the fact that he'd picked mushrooms for me was endearing. I realized he had heard as many rumors about me as I had about him. In my case, the rumors (and mushrooms) were closer to the truth. The chanterelles were to be my final savory course in the eating marathon. I was seated to his right, his mother, spry and cheerful, sat at the head of the table next to her somewhat deaf older sister. Ginette kept on bouncing up and serving with unceasing energy.

We had to contend with so many courses that I lost track. The other guests and I oohed over the confit, which Ginette told us she had started to prepare two days before. Meanwhile, I had *canelle*, blintze-shaped dumplings. The table was filled with bottles plucked from the stoop—all wines that Jacques had had a part in developing, all reflecting varying degrees of carbonic maceration, including a twelve-year-old Maupertuis and the sublime, decade-old Ploussard of Overnoy. It was as if he were trying to make a point—they were Jacques's greatest hits. But while these wines were made for immediate consumption, they were also designed to age.

Jacques poured the 1990 for the others. He had hand-selected a three-year-old Pfifferling for me and my canelle. Don't get me wrong; I loved Pfifferling's Domaine de l'Anglore from Tavel, but I worshipped Overnoy. "Could I possibly have a glass as well?" I begged, feeling a little managed and pouty. Jacques was so playful that I didn't know if he was kidding me or not, but I realized he was quite serious. My desire to drink Overnoy seemed to muddle up Jacques's grand scheme for my wine pairings. I asked again. He conceded. In the end, to my palate, the Overnoy was a better match, as the vein of iron running through it meshed with the tomato sauce. Anyway, being a double-fisted drinker suits me, but I had to be vigilant.

There was nothing to pour my wine into, and no one was spitting. I realized that this was not about tasting; this was about drinking. Unfortunately, Amy had to drive, and I had to be cognizant enough to conduct a useful interview. I hate those situations where avarice must be tempered by professionalism. I had to proceed very carefully and take my portions in sips.

The day started at noon. Six hours later, we had gone through the ratatouille course, followed by *pintade*, flanked by caul-soaked cauliflower, followed by some more meat. Then I lost track. There was salad, eggs, and chanterelles, which I insisted on sharing, and about nine bottles for nine bodies, two of whom were not drinking. The noise and laughter level rose; I began to wonder if I was the only one still not tipsy. The day was closing, and there were a few questions I had yet to ask. So I put my fork down and asked about the addition that some in the natural world would like not to admit to using. "What do you think of the enzyme lysozyme?" I asked him.

His countenance darkened, as if I had disclosed some nasty secret about his mother. "I don't want to talk about it," he responded, shaking his head.

"Why?" I asked.

"I can't explain it. I don't like it, and I don't approve."

The level of his vehemence surprised me. This emotional response was as fierce as when he talked about another writer plagiarizing his words. But I had believed the support of lysozyme had come down from him. Thierry Puzelat, who had worked with Jacques, had talked about it with me openly. Even when I pressed Eric Texier about it, he said that because he works in small bunches, he just throws out the one that didn't work. "But," I had asked Eric, "if you worked in big vats, Eric, would you use it rather than lose your vintage?"

Eric admitted that if he were in that situation, he supposed he would use the enzyme. After all, winemaking naturally shouldn't mean you don't take medicine if you need it.

"But if you don't use it, is there any other way to save the vintage?" I now asked Jacques.

"There are other ways to deal with it," he said mysteriously. "But I won't tell you." He reiterated, "there is no recipe."

"Perhaps no recipes, but, Jacques, aren't there ideas? You can tell me what you did in that specific instance, no? Or at least tell me when this was?"

That he could. "In 1982, the vintage was beautiful. There was a lot of fruit, and there was piqûre lactique everywhere."

"And?" I asked.

"'Scientific' means you can do it again. It is very hard to admit when you work in this field that you don't have the answer. Go look for the answer in a diagnostic for psychological illness. You can't find it in wine books." And he started to laugh so hard, he was having a great time with me.

Jacques loved to play this cat-and-mouse game, but this was really frustrating. He wouldn't tell me.

"And, what did you do?" I asked one more time.

Luckily, I had the support of the others, who suddenly were interested in this conversation. Eager to play, Isabelle jumped up and held his arms behind him in a chair and started to mimic a taunt: "What did you do? What did you do, Jacques?" Then she yelled, "Ahleece, tickle him, tickle him!" It seemed to me as if the whole room started to chant, "Tickle him!"

Alice in Wonderland was at the tea party, but Alice didn't want to tickle anyone. Perhaps I just hadn't been drinking enough. With Isabelle playing with him as if he were five years old and Amy cooing, "Oh, Jacques, come on," I got him to talk through his laughter.

"I had an idea," he said, "and asked Monsieur Chauvet about it, and he said, 'Why not?'" The enologue stopped, like a mule in the field.

"And, what was that idea?" I asked.

He folded his arms. "I can't tell you. Because other people will try it, and it won't work."

He we go again, I thought—bring on the tickle. But after Amy intervened in her charming way, he continued.

"Some vats were fermenting well. I scooped out some of the marc from the good vats and added those skins to the vats that were failing. That worked. Winemaking is like rugby; you always have to look ahead."

All of that effort, just to find out he "fed" the funky vats some nutrients from the other vats? I felt let down, not because of the simplicity of the fix, but because it was no big secret. This was common sense. I did not understand this secrecy.

"Do you like stinky cheese?" he asked me, in an excellent move of deflection.

He might have asked does a bear love honey. I loved strong cheeses. Jacques retreated into his bedroom and emerged with crinkly white bags that he proceeded to unwrap. One can see the eccentricity in Jacques, perhaps in his beard, perhaps in his longer-than-usual nails, but keeping cheese in his room without refrigeration might be the biggest clue. He stored it there out of deference to his mother, who can't stand the *fromage* or its smell.

He unwrapped a Reblochon that had blushed red and microbial instead of its more usual tannish rind. There was no *politesse*. The cheese was way past its prime; it was as if the poor thing had *piqûre lactique* itself. Isabelle made great fun of him, and his mother looked long-suffering.

At this point, at the end of the meal, the table was littered with even more bottles, and yet we still weren't finished. Then the wine-maker, who had been so silent during the meal, brought out his wine for us to taste. Amy and I swapped a glance, then she ran to the car to fetch hers. This brought our bottle count up to eleven for nine people. She pulled the cork on her 2008 La Gramière, and she sipped with relief and a smile. "It's nice when even I can admit to loving a wine I've made," she said.

Her wine showed very well—a little chestnut, firm, and wild. Every wine on the table was made with some form of "method"; Amy's wine was done in open-top fermenters and had a normal fermentation, meaning the grapes were crushed and left to ferment. Her wine was singing, she said. I know what she meant; I had the same feeling when I tasted my Sagrantino.

Jacques examined Amy's Grenache with his nose and tongue. "It's well made," he proclaimed. Jacques was polite; he gave her absolution when he said, "If you export your wine, you have to add sulfur."

The *vin naturel* world isn't evangelical, but there is sometimes something sweetly encouraging about it. Like when Andrea Calek had gently asked Amy, "Did you ever try to make wine without sulfur? Why not?"

Pierre Overnoy, who helped form the Association des Vins Naturels, said that it is important to encourage people to work toward a natural path. The point is not to gain converts, but to help people make the wine that is in their soul. Pierre told François Morel, "There are those who work organically in the vines and add a little sulfur as they learn to do without. We shouldn't exclude them [from the organization] as they're moving in the right direction. On the other hand, if there's someone who is certified organic who puts huge doses of sulfur in the wine, that's just not admissible. What's important is that they are going in the right direction."

Amy could have very well been included in such an organization since her goal was increasingly to use less and less. She could absolutely belong to "the cool kids" if she wanted to or could be just as cool if she didn't.

With a steady hand, Ginette started to scoop out *œufs à la neige* (eggs in snow), a dessert that before this moment, always left me cold. Ginette's version was a swirl of rich and light and surprise. As she spooned the floating soft meringues onto the sunny-colored *crème anglaise* on her son's plate, she told Amy that every morning, Jacques gets up and goes into his study and stays all day. "I have no idea what he does there," she said.

Whether in his room or in that town of one hundred or so people, his ability for aloneness seemed enviable.

We were not finished eating. God forbid. Out came the fresh-gathered garnet berries and celadon green figs with purpled flesh. I had ferreted some answers, but I wanted a little more. America was immersed in controversy about the word *natural* and its definition. Even so, the desire for wines made with nothing added or removed had skyrocketed. "What do you think of *vin naturel?*" I asked him. "And what has happened since you started to work?"

"I'm not really interested," he said. "It doesn't concern me."

"So this whole *vin naturel* movement originated with wines without sulfur," I said.

"Yes, that's it," he said. "To make wine without sulfur."

That was it. According to Jacques, I could search for the deeper meaning. I could stretch for the significance in Debord or Kant, but he was firm. As far as he was concerned (he who sired more than two thousand wines), *vin naturel* was born to make life without hangovers a reality.

While he had an adverse reaction to lysozyme, he never talked about the importance of farming. Yet Chauvet certainly did, for example, in *Le vin en question*: "You must come to the wine, 'reflection of its soil,' and with a minimum of chemicals, both in the soil as well as in the wine. I think one must attain the truth at last. I believe that this is the point. It is not easy! The older I grow, the more one wants to find truly natural wines, well-made wines."

Amy was self-conscious about her wines, but she need not have been. She was just more of a Chauvetist than a Néauportist.

As the lunch party came to a close, finally, we were allowed to leave without another morsel passing our lips. But there were final words from Jacques: "You know, Alice, when I heard you were coming, I was very happy. I wanted to meet you, but then I thought, 'Why is she coming here? I have nothing to tell her. She'll just be disappointed, because there is no answer. There is no answer.'"

And as I drove away with Amy, I pondered the conversation. Marcel Lapierre had once told me very solemnly, "Natural wines should be expressive of terroir and vintage. But a wine merely without sulfur and doesn't express anything, is not natural."

There was the philosophic split between Jacques and the people he had helped make wine. Nevertheless, I came away with an important reminder that the natural-wine movement was also about drinking. It was about the pure, pleasurable pursuit of drinking and conversation, and the reality that drinking often helps conversation flow. These wines were not about points or perfection or about color and body or structure. They were the kinds of wine that can bring charm and joy. Jacques did have the answer, after all.

CHAPTER 9

The American Vigneron

How on earth are you ever going to explain in
terms of chemistry and physics, so important a
biological phenomenon as first love?
—ALBERT EINSTEIN

Sometimes, I think my hunting for quirky winemakers is
merely an extension of my childhood delight for turning over
wet rocks in search of thin-skinned salamanders. But for a pig-
tailed, red-haired kid, the salamander search was a pastime: For
the winemaker, it is a mission.

On a damp and cool day in May, perfect East Coast salamander
weather, I was actually out West, in Healdsburg, California, and
had just pulled a beast of a gnarly celery root from my friend Marcy
Mallette's back yard. We deemed it too ancient to dice up, and so I
puttered around, helping my friend in the kitchen while, as usual,
guests bearing bottles produced a mini mountain of wines piled up

for dinner. I was looking forward to some old Gaglioppo I had carried north from Los Angeles. But little did I know, those bottles I brought were not going to be the surprise of the evening for the guests. After the beet salad came a local wine, Arnot-Roberts.

"This is your wine, the 2008 Clary Ranch Syrah?" I asked Nathan Roberts as I tried to register what this taste of California was in my mouth. Kevin Hamel was sitting next to me. He pulled it from my hands and poured himself a bit. As I mulled it over, I registered mint, clover, stem, spice, color, and horse. "Pretty neat!" I said and noted that this must have had low alcohol.

I found it lovely and delicious, but I suspected that some who were hooked on what is called the California style would run for the mouthwash. If this was a new direction for California, I was primed to write a retraction of my 2008 op-ed piece slamming California wines. Then I doubled back to the label . . . 11.5 percent? I was incredulous. After all, so many domestic wines were topping out at 15 percent or higher, which would have been the case if my Sagrantino hadn't been watered back. *But how did they come to even make a wine like that?* I thought.

The answer was deceptively simple, as I found out when I visited them a few months later, in August 2010. On the second day of a terribly hot spell that would terrorize the vintage, I drove into the dusty parking lot of the Arnot-Roberts old apple-processing barn in Forestville, Sonoma.

The winery was warm. Let's make that hot. With great relief, I was led to a narrow packing room with an air conditioner. There I was, around a barrel with fresh-faced Nathan Roberts and his equally fresh-faced, boyhood bud, Duncan Arnot Meyers, a friend since their Cub Scout days in Napa.

"You grew up in Napa, belonged to the Cub Scouts, and make wines like these?" I asked with great admiration. I had just tasted an angular Chardonnay and a vibrant Trousseau and had retasted that Clary Ranch Syrah. The Syrah had no fruit jam, but had horse sweat and muscle, zippy acidity and mint, structure and less than 12 percent alcohol.

They were embarrassed by the Cub Scouts and just did not understand how unusual their personal *élevage* was. In their perception, they grew up in a wine culture, so their evolution was normal. But I clarified my disbelief for them: "You had a Napa upbringing, the land of the-bigger-the-better, and now you make low-alcohol and low-intervention wines? No inoculations, acid, or tricks? Hell, you've got a Chardonnay in there still not finished from 2009. Don't people around here think you're freaks?"

Turns out this was a relatively new way of working for them. Their first vintage was in 2002. They inoculated. Their wines registered at high alcohol levels. Nathan said, "I think it was John Kongsgaard who gave us the confidence to go native with our fermentations. Duncan worked for him briefly during the 2003 harvest, and we have a lot of respect for his depth of experience. Most winemakers encouraged us to inoculate, because they told us it was safer and we'd have more control. John plainly assured us, in contrast to everyone else, that the risks are low."

The almost schoolboyish-looking men, biking fanatics, are among the most exciting new and brave faces on the California wine scene. Brave because no one made Syrah at such low alcohol levels and had the balls to refrain from putting fruit first.

The friends didn't pop out of the womb making wine in this lean and mean way. Their philosophical shift came about in the cooler 2005. They loved the quality of fruit the vintage gave them and, after a little soul searching, decided that instead of accentuating the flavor capacity of California wines, they'd work with it and pick when the grapes were more in balance, which meant earlier, sacrificing fruit for acid and a fresher wine.

I remember that during my talk at the Healdsburg library (the one that started my whole Sagrantino adventure), a local winemaker had asked me, "What can you do if you want to make a lower-alcohol wine with an earthier expression? How do you find the market?" I should have answered, "If you have to ask the question, you have your answer. Make conventional wines. That's all you can do." Instead I ended up suggesting that if they made the wine that suited them without worrying about the market, and they kept small, they'd find their drinker.

Like the best winemakers, Nathan and Duncan follow their own vision and stay small. If you are good, you will find a market. These two men know it. With only fifteen hundred cases to sell, they sell them all.

They also explained that they traveled and talked to their favorite winemakers, studied how the skilled people in the Northern Rhône handled the juice, and took their lessons to heart.

"But others around you do the same thing," I argued. "Several people around these parts cite the winemaker, Thierry Allemand, who makes restrained and sometimes even austere Cornas, as their god, but then make superripe, market-driven stuff."

Duncan said with a shrug, "Our palates shifted westward towards the ocean."

I wasn't sure that this explanation told me anything other than they just listened to their intuition, not only about winemaking but also about land. I had always believed that there was California terroir. With the state's long strip of land hugging the coast and its jumble of volcanic rock, soil, and old sea bed, how could there not be? Which is why Duncan and Nathan sought out Clary Ranch, a vineyard close to Tomales Bay, which has been described as a windblown, fog-tormented area with denuded hillsides. I could use that in my tasting note to explain its cold-weather flavors of cola, clover, and spice. The foot-trodden 2006 was picked on November 3 at 21.05 Brix, the ripest the grapes have ever plumped out to.

Our talk turned to gossip about the current buzz about the word *natural* and the second San Francisco Natural Wine week under way. I was very curious to know what they thought of some of the wines being poured during the celebration. Like me, they had doubts. Duncan said it this way: "There should be a distinction between doing or adding something to a wine to prevent a loss and doing or adding something to a wine to make it taste like something it is not. I have had this discussion with a few who are passionate about this topic and I was surprised that they all felt that those exceptions could be made. Wines bottled with that type of intervention, to me, exclude themselves from being called natural, but I am not sure the winemaker should be deprived of that title, if those exceptions only rarely occur. I suppose that is still a cop-out, but I am a pretty tolerant person by nature."

So, it comes down to the commitment to intention. According to Pierre Overnoy, one should be encouraging. A truly natural wine, most natural-wine proponents agree, is not possible in every year, but no one ever needs gum arabic, tannin addition, micro-oxygenation or strong doses of sulfur at every stage. There are limits. What's more, I questioned that some of the winemakers included in the natural-wine group were large enough to be factory-like. But, significantly, there was no stated philosophy about yeast or a commitment about sulfur. So, I blogged my feelings and raised my questions.

Soon, a fight broke out on The Feiring Line. Winemaker Robert Sinskey wrote, defending his farming, his biodynamics, his 180 acres, and all of his employees:

> We allow nature to drive our winegrowing and winemaking. However, we believe in producing a wine that is sound when it goes in the bottle so the work in the vineyard is reflected in the finished wine. We are not perfect. Dig deep enough and you will find inconsistencies and contradictions, as you will find with every "natural" producer. Once a human is involved in the farming and winemaking process, we are no longer working in a natural environment, we can emulate natural systems though every decision we make in the process is an intervention.

Though I never cited Sinskey as one of the winemakers who didn't belong, he reacted as if I had. Trying to explain himself, that simple word *however* spoke loudly. Sinskey aimed to make a "sound" wine, implying that a "natural" wine was not sound. As if a natural wine were necessarily a wine gone amuck. He was knocking the club of which he wanted to align with. With Sinskey, it was a little fudge-able. Because the real crime is when industrial and conventional wines pass themselves off as artisanal and natural. Sinskey, on the other hand, was sustainable, and he practiced biodynamic farming. Perhaps his wines weren't overprocessed; perhaps they were natural enough. But given his size and his attitude—and most likely his attitude toward yeast and sulfur—his wines just could not be put in the same category as an Eric Texier, an Oriol Illa, an Andrea Calek, or some like-minded Californians. His is just not that kind of commitment.

Not everyone can be radical and embrace that tipping point— no or low sulfur. Without that philosophy deep in his core, Sinskey could find no entry into this radical world of natural.

Perhaps *naked wine* is a more protective term than *natural wine* in the end. *Naked* sings of vulnerability. It means exposed, a willingness to risk all. While I can imagine the labels—depicting a man clutching a fig leaf to his privates—should the bottles get past the Alcohol and Tobacco Tax and Trade Bureau (TTB), it might just be hard to hide behind that one simple word.

For quite some time, when people asked me for California wine recommendations, I started to stammer trying to think quickly about who made wine that I liked to drink, and came up with Steve Edmunds. For the past thirty years, he had been making wine without bowing to fashion and, since 2000, had done so in an increasingly natural way. Change started about 2007, when all of a sudden, I could add a whole two fistfuls of people working with a commitment to wine made with grapes and only a touch of sulfur as needed. The Brandts and their Donkey and Goat (having learned at the knee of Eric Texier), Hank Beckmeyer of La Clarine Farm, Kevin Kelley of Natural Process Alliance (NPA) and Salinia, Gideon Bienstock of Clos Saron, a nice little project by the name of Lioco (also with Kevin Kelley as winemaker), and the Coturris in Sonoma are at the top of the heap for me. As of 2011, I see a new crop of winemakers sprouting their first vintages. They will swell these ranks. If not a paradigm shift, they will at

least broaden the foundation of winemakers who take natural se-
riously. But still, what was I going to do about my desire for an
American vigneron? How would I make room for the likes of
Duncan and Nathan?

The next day, I decided to set something right and to make a visit
that was long overdue. It was a mere ninety-six degrees or so. I
grabbed my friend Marcy and drove to Coturri in Glen Ellen, clear
on the other side of the county. Baking in the heat, the landscape
seemed friendlier to cattle ranching than to grapes. We wended
our way on the back lanes, past brush and the pipe-cleaner-thin,
copper-barked trees.

Tony Coturri (with brother, vineyard manager Phil) had the
winery bonded in 1979, aiming to make wine the way their father
learned from their Tuscan grandfather. The only difference was
that they now fermented in small one-ton redwood tanks instead
of two and they use more whole clusters. I'd met Tony several
times in New York City and found he looked like his younger hippie self. He wore the same scraggly ponytail and frilly, unkempt
beard as in his youth, but now they were fringed with silver. He's
shy, but fierce, and when he talked about punching down the
grapes with his hand, his voice showed emotion. I thought of the
time Kevin pressed down on the Sagrantino grapes with his hands,
as if to feel their heartbeat. Like his wine, little had changed. Tony
believes that the human contact is important in the wines he
wants to make, and I swear, I felt that way every time I jumped
into the tank of Sag grapes and felt the life of fermentation on
my skin.

Tony's wines had been in my consciousness since the mid-1980s, when their bottles were often relegated to the "organic" section—a pathetic rack of a few wines. Where other bottles were treated with more respect and rested on their sides, far from the sun that shone through windows, these bottles often stood up, unprotected from the sunlight. This is bad for any wine, but it is worse for unsulfured examples. I confess that I dismissed Tony's wine as well-meaning hippie juice. It was an unfair opinion. After all, I was a little hippie wannabe myself, too young at the time to be part of the movement, but yearning to grow up to be free. That movement ushered in a glorious era for music and was the foundation for the stirring of the food renaissance. Perhaps because of wine's being an industry and co-opted by big business, its renaissance lagged behind. In the early days, organic took precedence over "good wine," but his understanding, even then, that not all wines were natural, was ahead of his time. He wanted to do something different. His "nothing added, and nothing taken away" approach was ahead of its time. The Coturris were late in receiving their due.

It wasn't until Jenny brought them into Jenny & François as their first American winery that I had an opportunity to reconsider the Coturris' merit. I was at a New York City party and had spent quality time with the Coturri Carignan 2004. This grape, which sells cheaply in the United States, is the same variety as the pricey Priorats, but even though it does splendidly on the West Coast of the United States, there Carignan is considered low rent. What surprised me is that I didn't just tolerate the wine; I truly enjoyed it. Call me impressionable (I've been called worse), but I thought it tasted like California, whatever that means—wild, unbridled, and friendly.

This was crazy. Tony and *vin naturel* were separated at birth—
by six thousand miles. The Coturri winery had been organic and
sulfur free—read hard-core natural—since 1979. That was a clear
two years before François Morel started his *sans soufre* wine bar
and before the gang in Beaujolais gathered any momentum. Tony
was a leader who had no idea there were followers. He had no idea
he wasn't working in a vacuum until he went to Paris only a decade
ago and visited a *caviste* (wine shop) that a friend had recom-
mended (he can't remember which *caviste*) because it had bottles
it called natural wines. He discovered not Marcel Lapierre, but the
Paolo Bea Sagrantino, in an odd twist of irony. Tony was still
struggling to fit in, but in that moment, he perceived that perhaps
he belonged to something bigger. Until Tony joined up with Nicolas Joly's Return to Terroir group and then with Jenny, he had no
idea just how large and important the piece of tapestry he fit into.

Marcy and I rolled past conventional vines along the way, and
I wondered if those uninspiring ones could be Coturri. Sure
enough, when we saw a stretch of vines with welcoming arms and
messy soil, the ownership was obvious. Welcome to Coturri.
Marcy drove us into the land, winery, and home, past old and trel-
lised Zinfandel vines, with their large canopy of leaves. We parked
and walked up to the house. Because Tony was away on business,
his son, Nic, as tall and skinny as a new spruce, greeted us. He was
in his midtwenties and looked maybe thirteen, yet he was the face
of the future and taking on more of his dad's role.

Before the temperature went incendiary, I wanted to walk the
vines. Phil Coturri, Tony's brother, is the viticulturist who started
the first organic vineyard management company in America.
When Nic wanted to show us his pride, his garden, I wondered if
he had more of his uncle's genetic disposition.

"One thousand tomato plants," Nic said.

"Honey," I answered, "you don't have a garden; that's a god-damned farm."

Nic's fruits and vegetables were carefully plotted in back of the Zinfandel. It was like an Eden, so much so that I expected to see a rattler on the tree of life.

Contrasting the well-organized piece of garden design was the wreck in the cave. Dug into the cool hillside, the place had no temperature control. Barrels were snuggled on top of each other as close as a cattle-stuffed boxcar. The storage room was just as cluttered. There we struggled for a convenient place to stand and taste. "My grandfather made wine the way his grandfather made wine in Tuscany," young Nic said, pouring some 2009 Chardonnay into our glasses. I liked it, even though I don't usually find domestic Chardonnay in any way appealing. The 2008 Carignan showed a smoked-lamb character from the vintage that was plagued by forest fires. Sure, it was smoky, but unlike most California winemakers, the Coturris did not erase the smoke with reverse-osmosis machines. They accepted the smoky aspect as the vintage. Then there was that violet-like 2005 Cabernet. I'm a sucker for purple flowers. For all of those years, the Coturris risked family finances on making wine stubbornly hard-core and true to its nature and place.

"My father tells me that years back," said Nic, "there was a San Francisco wine store that refused to carry the wine because they were afraid that without sulfur, the bottles would explode and send bacterial contamination all over the shop." I thought that this was the same kind of ignorant statement used in arguments against natural wine. But bottles made without sulfur don't have to explode. They merely need to be treated with care.

The Coturris have waited thirty-plus years for their wines to gain acceptance and for people to understand how to handle the bottles. Even though their wines might be made without temperature control, these wines and other no-sulfur wines do need cool temperatures for transport and storage. No sulfur means the wines need special handling. Moreover, there is bottle variation, as each wine is a live entity. Sometimes there might be a little spritz from carbon dioxide (this is where a decanter or a wide-mouth pitcher comes in handy). And as Jules Chauvet said, one shouldn't be afraid of a little gas in the wine.

In each vintage, there will be similarities because the grapes come from the same plot of land. But the differences from year to year can be expected, because each year, nature delivers its seasonal message in a different way. Hopefully, the wines are at least lively and interesting, and often, they can be extremely exciting. A word of caution, however: In the world of natural, there are good winemakers and not so good. This is exactly as it is in the world of conventional wines.

When I had left the Coturris' vineyard that afternoon, it was with a case of open bottles to share with friends at Marcy's that night, as well as a new appreciation and context of a longer history of U.S. *vin naturel* than I—and probably most others—had supposed.

I would be fibbing if I didn't admit that Marcy, who had grown up hunting morels in Nebraska (but found her soul in Northern California), doesn't throw the best dinner parties in Healdsburg. And after our hot visit in the Coturri vineyards, I was happy to be back at her place under the star-studded sky, sitting, drinking, and eating in her backyard. The guests all wore flip-flops, and Kevin Hamel had made fun of my lace-ups. "Will someone please take this girl to a drugstore and get her proper footwear?" he had asked.

Yes, I was out of the shtetl, but still felt at peace. That New York irony had been tempered, my sharp edges felt a little softer, and that night, unbelievably, I was tasting the local wines. The soirée challenged the most idyllic Provençal evenings, and I realized that I was starting to give myself over to California.

As the night moved on, we sat underneath a fig tree groaning with unripe fruit. Guests sopped up the last of their Alaskan salmon BLT in the finally cool night air. I reached into the pileup of wines near the ice bucket for the next sip. I selected one and poured it around, returning to the end of the long alfresco dinner table. Hardy Wallace took a tentative taste of Coturri's 2005 Cabernet and exclaimed with a broad smile, "Ooh, that's sure some hippie-juice!" He was certain the wine had a significant retro taste, within spitting distance of a Haight-Ashbury head shop.

Hardy is a young, manic, and vibrant cherub who arrived in Northern California from Atlanta (though a born New Englander) to live out a dream. The dream was induced when he won a very high profile contest to be the social media guru for a Kendall Jackson winery. He knocked out the competition with his brains and goofball charm. After his six months, however, he really found his dream job, with Kevin Kelley, the winemaker whose grapes I had trod—cheated on, I suppose—when my Sagrantino was in process. Hardy's palate was more aligned with said hippie juice than techno-wines. I kept on trying to analyze his expression to see what he really thought about the wines. I knew if I had brought along the rosé or even the Chardonnay, he'd have been as won over

as Marcy and I had been. These particular wines I brought were
not for everyone. In general, the Coturris are not for everyone, but
I realized that at five thousand cases total, they didn't have to be.

Those around me now tried to make sense out of the wine. The
Coturri Cabernet had some nail-polish-remover-like volatile acidity, a note that modern wines try to expunge. I tried to gauge
Nathan Roberts's impression; he wasn't sure. I said firmly, "Like
them or not, they are a national treasure, just like Lopez de Heredia in Rioja and Bartolo Mascarelo in Barolo, and you know how
much I love those wines." As I said those words, I was ashamed.
How had I ignored the Coturris? Was it just because of my pre-
conceived notion of wine in America that I didn't take the time to
find out what was on home turf? I didn't know there was someone
like them, carving their own way with dogged commitment to create an authentic example of America.

People can debate ad nauseam the tendentious use of the word
natural for wine. In a piece for *Slate* and in a personal letter to me,
my colleague Michael Steinberger wrote about the challenge of
using this word: "People using the term 'natural wines,' need to
come up with a much more convincing justification for its use, or
they need to find a better, less loaded term to describe the wines."

This may indeed be true, but more significant to me is the lack
of an English equivalent for *vigneron*. The reason is telling: The
concept of a singular person who both farms and makes his or her
own wine is an unusual one in the United States. When I was immersed in my Sagrantino project, I had felt this separation of
labor—of farming and vinifying—on a visceral level, and it still

frustrates me that it is accepted as the standard. In the French and Spanish grassroots definitions of *natural*, some clauses address this separation of farming and vinifying. In Spain, the Productores de Vinos Naturales guidelines spell out the relationship between farming and vinifying: "The grower is the winemaker." France's Association des Vins Naturels charter goes further: "The winemaker member . . . is a farmer, filled with passion for his terroir and his craft." Could I imagine a Jordi Sanfeliu or a Laureano Serres or an Eric Texier or a Frank Cornelissen without rugged hands from pruning? The relationship between the land and what is in the bottle would be severed if the wine became a packaged product. This is not to say the love is gone if the winemaker doesn't grow the grapes; a family can still love a child who was brought up in the care of a governess. But the emotional attachment is different.

California is so pricey—Napa can fetch upwards of 500,000 dollars an acre for land with vines—yet some people, even those who did not buy early (like the Coturris), sometimes find lonely or unfashionable nooks in which to set up shop. They might not be getting rich, but that isn't their aim. If these brave and single-minded souls proliferate, an accurate English word for the likes of Benyamin Cantz might be created.

As a lapsed orthodox Jew whose first taste of wine was kosher and sweet mixed with seltzer, I am often the one requested to show up with a bottle of super-kosher vino. During these moments, I scrounge around and am often completely disappointed by the mostly deplorable choices—insults, I'm afraid. My measuring stick is what can I tolerate as opposed to what I'm crazy about. At one time in Eastern Europe, many Jews had vineyards and wineries and made wine, but Hitler took care of that. So, from my point of view, the taste of the Old World kosher wines were wiped out, and sweet wines took over. There was another abomination, flash pasteurization. According to the ancient rabbis, a wine that is not *mevushal* cannot be opened up by a non-Jew.

A wine that is not *mevushal* must be handled at all times, from the winery equipment to the bottling to the opening, by a Sabbath observer. Thus, non-*mevushal* wine is not even safe in my own hands. A *mevushal* bottle has economic worth; these wines are in demand at parties and restaurants where orthodox Jews might not be serving.

In my research, I had come across someone, a character named Benyamin Cantz, who lived a short sprint above his four acres of certified organic, dry-farmed vines in the Santa Cruz Mountains. His Four Gates Winery was a one-man operation that specialized in non-*mevushal* wines. That did it. On the plane. Out there. I had to see this with my own eyes. So on the same spring trip when I visited Marcy and had pulled out the gnarled celery root and first sampled that Clary Ranch Syrah, I also ventured out to meet Cantz.

I had texted José: "What do you think, road trip?"

It was a short two-hour excursion from José's bayside apartment in Tiburon. Tanking up on coffee and forgetting to eat, we ended up on a twisty road climbing a petite mountain. Santa Cruz has history. There were some notable wineries—most notably Ridge, Rhys, and Calera—in that range of mountains. The region was also historic. The Burgundian Paul Masson, who worked hero-ically to develop an important wine industry here, set up vines in the late 1800s. He sold off just after the Great Depression to Mar-tin Ray (who, by the way, was responsible for creating geographical distinctions for California vineyards and was controversial for not only being a difficult character but for making wines without sulfur, though he did use yeast after prohibition). The Paul Masson name was subsequently sold and, unfortunately, became associated with plonk. The brand was best known for its 1970s marketing association with Orson Welles, who promised: "We will sell no wine before its time."

"Where are we?" José asked as we drove along the windy road.

"We're supposed to look for a shrine. Is that it?" I asked, pointing to a flower-strewn roadside marker.

"Maybe," José said. We stopped and contemplated.

"It is!" I said, seeing something. "Go right." My Hebrew was intact enough that I could read the words written on a piece of driftwood in front of a small path. *Bruchim Habaim*, which distills down to "welcome" but translates into "blessings on those who come."

Riding up the tree-bordered path, I was transported back to a hotel in Monsey, New York. A summer and a family intact. Me in a sunsuit, running from the sun.

"I'm hungry," José said.

"He'll have lunch for us," I said. "Just hold on."

We drove past two slopes of vines and then came face-to-face with a horse in a blanket. Shortly after parking, we saw a tall man, somewhere near sixty, come out to greet us. He was wearing a baseball cap instead of a yarmulke. He moved slowly, as if he owned time.

Benyamin's foray into winemaking must have been guided by a higher authority. He never consciously had wine on the brain; nor did he feel he had a great palate. His story started in 1971, when this former San Fernando Valley boy, former peace marcher, and art history major moved to the Santa Cruz Mountains to watch over the property of his Santa Cruz University art professor. Surprisingly, he found he was smitten with the area's beauty—the land was six hundred feet above sea level—as well as the farming and the caring for the goats. Except for the animals, he was, in 2010, the only full-time resident on the mountain, but back in 1979, there was a fellow tenant who farmed marijuana. "He planted Chardonnay vines as, shall we say, cover crop," Benyamin quipped. "The tenant eventually left, but the vines remained. I watched over them."

Benyamin became increasingly observant, and by 1990, without ever having tasted, let alone drunk, any of the world's great wines, he became obsessed with vinification. His motivation wasn't the idea of making a New World stand-in for Richebourg or Chinon, but for making a simple wine over which to chant Sabbath and holiday kiddush. He supplemented that Chardonnay with 3.5 acres of Cabernet Franc, Merlot, and Pinot Noir planted on sandstone, limestone, and clay soils. By Jewish law, he had to wait until the fourth leaf appeared to use his fruit. In 1996, he vinified his first commercial vintage. His yield is teensy: 1.5 to 2 tons per acre, and he makes only four hundred cases. He takes a do-nothing approach in the vineyard, not because of a philosophy but because he is one person.

"You could use some clover to break up the soil up and let it breathe a bit," I observed to him. The soil, which had never been tilled, seemed parched and needed more aeration to make it spongy.

We walked up the hill from his vines and sat on Adirondack chairs. It felt as if we were watching the grapes grow. As a wired New Yorker, this was a pace I could personally never handle, something I realized about myself even as a little girl who felt claustrophobic with the quietness of the Sabbath. José, usually talkative, was quiet as Benyamin and I talked about life, religion, and winemaking. I have never met a commercial winemaker who works so in isolation. He lives there with horses, geriatric goats, golden dog, chickens, Talmud, and vines.

When Benyamin took us over to see his winery, it seemed more like a weaver's studio. I warned José not to touch anything. I had tried to explain to him earlier that because he, José, wasn't Jewish, and because I wasn't religious, we couldn't touch anything that had to do with the wine; otherwise, the winery would cease to be kosher. Benyamin uses a basket press the size of a large White Mountain hand-cranked ice-cream maker. He also has one of the more Lilliputian crusher/de-stemmers I've seen. It is made from redwood, with gleaming metal dowels. To hell with Monsey. All of a sudden, I was somewhere in the refreshing Carpathians, turning over rocks on the hunt not only for salamanders but also for sprites, and I could smell the wild strawberries and the freshly milked cows. "Please don't touch anything, or we'll have a disaster," Benyamin reminded.

I was raised in the kind of household that precut the toilet paper before Shabbos, and I found it infuriating that my history didn't grandfather me in. Nevertheless, I obediently kept my hands to myself. José's stomach audibly rumbled; mine followed. It was getting late, and we needed food, and I began to wonder if a Benyamin lunch was at all a possibility. But we didn't come all this way not to sample Four Gates, so we traversed the foliaged path to an unkempt cottage, a bachelor-like affair infused with good-natured absentmindedness. We entered through the kitchen; detritus was left behind from his morning of cooking. In one open room was the rustic kitchen and dining/living room. An English version of the Kabbalah was splayed out on his table. The wine-maker, it would seem, was more interested in reading than in cleaning. Then I heard the stealthy padding of little feet. Confused, I chose my seat. That's when a small red head peeked out of the draped tablecloth.

"Oh, that's Goldie Green," said Benyamin. That's because she's golden and she lays green eggs." He didn't laugh. Neither did the chick, who wore the kind of expression that told me she'd be happier to hop on Benyamin's seat and start to read about divine intellect or divine emotions than to leave the premises. Yet, guests were here and the chicken was on an exit path. Guiding her outside, Benyamin explained, "You see, she's really not a chicken."

We needed to taste the wines, and I was feeling uncomfortable because José's stomach was growling so loudly. But from the first sip of 2006 Cabernet Franc, he forgot for a second. "This is great. Alice, did you taste this?"

Because he was orthodox, he had never tasted the world's best anything when it came to wine, including Cabernet Franc. But even though, or maybe even because, he had no idea what the benchmarks were—meaning in this case no Loire Valley Chinon or Bourgueil or Saumur-Champigny—Benyamin made something extremely true. Not only that, but he also had the touch in working without sulfur. A friend, Rabbi Levine, is allergic to sulfur, so Benyamin had made a special cuvée for him. The 2007 Rabbi Levine unsulfured wine (not for commercial sale) kicked ass. Then there was a 1996 Chardonnay without sulfur. Fresh! Lemon and butter. Yes, way too oaky for me, but I swear there was something alive in that bottle. The man had talent. The kosher wine world would be a better place if he'd increase production, but he is now wary of doing that with bought fruit. In 2009, he was asked to make some Napa Cabernet for a friend from purchased grapes. The results, according to the winemaker, weren't pretty. "I now own acid," he said. "Something I never needed to buy, just in case I encounter grapes like that again."

We had to go. We were starving. José was about to pass out. We made apologies. I couldn't have my chauffeur passing out on me.

"But I made lunch!" Benyamin, a bit of a *luftmensch*, said. He had forgotten all about the pots on his stove. He spooned out for us king's portions of a very delicious, endearing, and humble pasta puttanesca. José ate two platefuls. Gratefully.

In the end, the only thing that separated Benyamin from being the world's first kosher natural winemaker is the fear about going native. However, there are years when the fermentations happened spontaneously and if they just start quickly enough, he is smart enough not to get in their way. "It was G-d's wine," he said. "And it was delicious."

While his town was maybe thirty minutes from the fashionable college town of Santa Cruz, others choose to set up shop far away from the nearest good loaf of bread. This is what Hank Beckmeyer and his wife, Caro, did when they moved to the somewhat unfashionable (some might say unlivable) area in the Sierra Foothills.

I discovered Hank, or should I say, Hank discovered me through my blog, where he showed up frequently. One day, he asked, "Can I send you wine?" He was inquisitive; he had been a musician, and he and his wife raised goats, everything pointed to similar sensibilities. But still, I was apprehensive because it was a stranger asking you to read his stack of poems. Now I liked him, but what if I didn't like the wines? I would have to tell him the truth, I decided. The bottles arrived with some extra tidings. "If you hate the wine, at least you'll love the cheese," he wrote in a note.

I took one sip after another. Earthy, fruit, tannin, all unmasked and all transparent, and I felt life and expression. When I see this in a wine, I am compelled to see where it came from. That is why I braved the drive to nowhere to find out what motivated a Michigan-born, Florida-bred guy to become one of America's few vignerons.

Just an hour east of Sacramento, I hooked a right out of a small, Podunk-ish town of Placerville, downshifted, and drove up to the sky. Through the clearing of pine and oak, sticking out of the side of a foothill about a thousand feet above sea level, I saw jagged rock—not just rock, but granite. This wasn't too far away from where the Gold Rush kicked off. I thought, *Where some are fools for gold, I am fool enough to be a fool for granite*. God, I just love wine grown on granite. It was everywhere, jutting out of waterfalls, bursting from the flesh of the hill; my terroir-o-meter went off the charts. Maybe the legendary wine consultant André Tchelistcheff was right, that the Sierra Nevada might have the best terroir in the state.

Finding Hank's place was easy, and I was soon in third gear, driving up on his scrubby land. When he saw my car approaching, Hank lumbered toward me. He had the inquisitive eyes of a Siberian husky, his face looked sort of like Tim Robbins, and he had the vocal timbre of Jerry Jeff Walker. I left my bag in the car, and we first walked through his vines, where feral chicken escapees from the chicken coop ran through the plants, pecking off bugs. Scrappy-looking vines, some under net to keep the birds away, swept up the hills, planted willy-nilly.

"I wanted them to look as if they've always been there," he explained. They do. "It's more of an art project with commercial leanings," he added.

As I walked among the vines, my feet cracked the wild sage, releasing the intense and refreshing, cleansing scent into the air. Over near the goats, he had built a his-and-her barn. On one side of the barn was his wife Caro's cheese-making facility and milking hut; on the other side, the tiniest winery with old barrels where he made his entire four-hundred-case production, about the same as Benyamin's. It seems that Hank's dad, who was a doctor, set the stage when he advised his son not to follow in his footsteps. "It was the only advice I ever followed," he told me.

Hank ditched education, moved with his guitar to Brooklyn, landed a position in the band Half Japanese, and toured. He eventually landed in the music production business in Hamburg. On a trip to Cannes, he tasted a Bandol from producer Lucien Peyrouse, Domaine Tempier. He aligned his taste buds with that particular kind of wine, low intervention, and made it his model. His first vintage was made in his German kitchen from German grapes, and Caro made her first cheese in the closet. They plotted a change of life to take their obsessions professional. They thought of France, but Hank was eager to return home, so they thought of Sonoma—better food and more people—but the real estate was bone-breakingly expensive. When he saw the ten-acre property with interesting climate and soil that reminded him of the Languedoc, that sealed the deal.

"I needed to grow my own vines," Hank said. To do one without the other is half the job. Sure, it is fun to bulk grapes and use different vineyards, but it doesn't have the same importance or provide the same emotional attachment." He was echoing my own feelings about what had kept me disconnected from the New World paradigms of wine.

Goat feeding time was upon us, and Caro was already spreading grain and talking to her "girls." Hank stood back with me and pointed out the billies. "In two months," he said, "around mating time, they start to get really smelly, filled with pheromones. The stinkiest ones get the most girls." Leaving me to ponder my own proclivity toward men who smell like white truffles, he went to join Caro and was swarmed by the animals.

While I know many devotees of biodynamics, and many wines I drink are farmed in that way, I don't believe it is the only path. It is just one way. Following the methods of Masanobu Fukuoka is another. *One Straw Revolution* had its effect on Hank, as well as on Frank Cornelissen and Eric Texier. The winemaking philosophy of "do little" resonates also in the vineyard. Fukuoka is more like natural wine: There are no rules; it is a way of life and an ethos. "It seemed to address the same issues as biodynamics, but without religious overtones," Hank explained. "It encapsulates the same ideas, but is unburdened by the feeling that farmers need to always 'do' things to make the plants grow."

I uncovered an old interview with the farmer Fukuoka in *Mother Earth News*. He said that his process didn't mean that scientific knowledge should be dismissed.

That course of action is simply abandonment, because it ignores the cycle of dependence that humans have imposed on an altered ecosystem. If a farmer does abandon his or her "tame" fields completely to nature, mistakes and destruction are inevitable. The real path to natural farming requires that a person know what unadulterated nature is, so that he or she can instinctively understand what needs to be done (and what must not be done) to work in harmony with its processes. If he were alive today, Fukuoka additions to the natural-wine debate would be a gift.

The year 2010 might be remembered as the year that natural wine debuted in the mainstream. That was also the year the genre was attacked—hard, often, and brilliantly. When Robert M. Parker used the word *scam* to describe the natural-wine movement, he was joined by others in that almost xenophobic reaction. David Schildknecht agreed:

> The implication of the term "natural wine" isn't just that for it to mean anything at all, there must be a category of "UN-natural wine. Surely most of us recognize in many areas, not merely wine, the extent to which spurious dichotomies of this sort, especially when conjoined with a Manichean mind set on the part of zealous partisans, can be perniciously misleading.

With all sincere respect due to Schildknecht, he was referring to the word rather than the category, but his use of the words *spurious, Manichean,* and *perniciously* is so, well, *Daily News* sensationalist, even though I know he is not that kind of man. These words dance well with a word like *scam,* used by Schildknecht's boss, Robert Parker. Reading Schildknecht's comments, I could imagine I was listening to Sean Hannity and not a discourse on people who like to drink and make certain wines.

The obsession to find a bulletproof label for the wines seems obsessively petty and deflective. Who cares whether a wine is called natural or naked or real or plain? Sure, if you like, seek out these wines because they politically and philosophically resonate with a personal credo about the environment and food. But no matter what they are called, isn't the germane motivation to drink these wines not about being politically correct, not about whether they are in fashion, but about their taste? Granted, not being tricked into buying a spoof wine instead of a real one is a conundrum if the name is abused. The answer, however, goes back to an old clutch of behaviors: asking, reading, and experiencing. I fear there is no shortcut.

One of the most beautiful sentences about wine was said aloud over the famed La Tâche vineyard in Burgundy: "You can deny God, but you can't deny that the sun rises." I feel the same way about wines that surprise you. One of the purest reactions to a natural wine came from Frank Bruni, the past restaurant critic of the *New York Times*. I first met Frank through our mutual friend in Rome. We were at one of his favorite Roman restaurants, Monti, and we were each charged with choosing a wine. With two very different bottles on the table, I was able to see him taste, and I was determined to show him some tricks when he returned to New York City. A month or two after that dinner, both of us were attending a lox party at the home of our friend, food writer Melissa Clark, in Brooklyn. I brought a wine from the Loire; the bottle had a clown label on it and was called Patapon. It cost a huge eleven dollars. It was in my budget and was made from the Pineau d'Aunis grape. "Here," I said to Frank, "try this."

I'll never forget his face; he gave it a sip. He burst out laughing. "Alice! What the hell is that?" he asked me.

What more can you ask of a wine than provoking a huge smile from the drinker? The next day, he sent an e-mail: "Where can I buy that?"

That wine was an Aldous Huxley *Doors of Perception* moment for him. Frank proved to have very specific tastes, perhaps more forgiving than mine; he started to reach for the wines that were more natural, discovering a love for high-acid whites and reds. He might have found them on his own, but during the years he had spent in Italy, finding natural wines had been a tough task. For example, the slow-food movement didn't even know the equivalent in wine existed. The wines were impossible to stumble upon, unless you knew to keep turning over those rocks.

Another friend, the guitarist Anthony Wilson, played with Diana Krall. As a California-based dude, he used to have a fair amount of hyped juice, but that all started to change when he was influenced by Kermit Lynch's book, *Adventures on the Wine Route*, specifically, reading about Marcel Lapierre. "Kermit's newsletter talked about the fragility of these wines" said Anthony, "and would always be very explicit about the fact that they needed to be stored properly. I could easily taste that they were different from other wines, and I adored their purity and intensity, but hadn't had enough experience with wine to really know what set them apart. It was only after many years, and especially after drinking too many modern, overcrafted, spoofy wines, that I returned to the kinds of wines I had started with: old-world, traditional, more restrained."

He dates his aha! moment to 2008, when a Muscadet from Domaine de la Pépière showed up at a Labor Day party. "I was blown away by the wine," Anthony told me. "It was everything I wanted in wine and rarely found. It was another world: pure, mineral, intense, but also pretty, beguiling. I only learned later that these wines I was beginning to crave (and the Morgons that I started drinking back in 1994) could be grouped under the 'natural wine' umbrella. Since 2008, I haven't looked back."

Anthony has become a true believer. I have volumes of texts from him when he was on the 2009 Krall tour. Typical was this: "In Brussels? Hook me up!" From Amsterdam, France, Italy, Croatia, even Warsaw, I plugged him into his *vin naturel* connection, when he didn't have his own. His enthusiasm spilled over to the guys on the tour bus, one bottle of natural wine at a time. "They don't want anything else," he wrote. In Paris, Krall's agent gave them a case of Bordeaux. "Painful," Anthony wrote to me.

I understood well. While Anthony Wilson was more militant than Frank Bruni, all of us were challenged by the tastes of market-driven, full-fruited, and spoof wines.

How, I wonder, can natural wines exist in America if they are done in the surrogate-mother way, the way I made that Sagrantino? While the Sagrantino had my feet and Kevin's hands, for me its soul will always be missing. It was, I admit, just a project.

If I'm ever going to step up and make my peace with America and the rest of the New World, I'm going to have to accept that not everyone can be a Coturri, a Cantz, or a Beckmeyer. Not everyone can grow his or her own grapes. As Americans move away from industry to art, our European friends, with their natural-wine guidelines, might have to find some wiggle room for the emerging, brave New World wines. Perhaps there will be special dispensation for wines made from purchased fruit. After all, it's not without some fine examples. Thierry Puzelat has a *négociant* line, made from bought grapes, that is no less natural than his domaine wines. The same is true for Eric Texier. The difference, of course, is that most of the European natural winemakers also farm even if they also buy grapes. This is important, even if it's only an acre.

Steve Edmunds does well, even though he doesn't have land, something he is painfully aware of. "I'm not a farmer," he said, "though I love to plant and tend my garden, and seem to have a decent feel for that. I let the bugs and critters have a little more of it than I'd like, and I can feel my murderous side emerge on occasion, mainly in response to the depredations of squirrels. I've learned enough, after nearly three decades, to size up what's going on in most vineyards I visit these days, to know how happy, or not, the vines are, and the rest of the things that grow in the vicinity, both animal and vegetable. After a few seasons, I began to know that the vineyard and I are not strangers."

The younger generations are onto it as well. While they don't own land at present, Duncan Meyers and Nathan Roberts spend time in the vineyards with pruning shears, as does Kevin Kelley. Maybe a particular American path can emerge.

My loyalties will always remain with those who work the vine *and* make the wine. No wonder. I was drawn to Americans who made their life as vignerons, even if they had to move elsewhere to do it. Like being in therapy, it's important to understand the problem, as understanding that you have a problem is the first step in overcoming it. A person needs to learn how to get intimate with a grape's home while not living with it. After all, there are all sorts of relationships: bicoastal ones, live-ins, non-live-ins, and even longtime affairs. It is not much of a stretch to apply this human concept to the vine.

My own relationship with the Sagrantino was confusing and confounding. Evers Ridgely asked me what I thought he should charge for that first vintage of Davero Sagrantino.

We were in his cool kitchen, and outside, August was raging in its heat. His question made me nervous. I was not good at business; it just did not run in my family. My father was the poorest lawyer I knew, with more pro bono than other work that filled the coffers.

My brother was a self-effacing, kindhearted cardiologist with a low mortality rate and holes in his shoes, and my mother was in the jewelry business, yet always acted as if she ran a charity.

So, where no one in my family ever appreciated the taste of wine, I come by my deep belief that the poor need healthy and nutritious food that they can afford. Moreover, humankind—including me, a close-to-the-bone freelancer—needs the equivalent in wine, even if it is a six- or seven-dollar bottle.

Wines made from the Holy Land, like La Tâche, with years of experience and demonstration, can be expensive, yes. But a vintage milked from young vines, from unchartered terroir? So I thought: This was Ridgely's first vintage from very young vines. The farming could have been better. The land's potential hadn't yet proved anything. What the wine did have, however, was a story. That made it marketable.

"No more than forty dollars," I offered, feeling as if I had set a huge price tag.

Ridgely had often told me that sustainable means sustainable for the farmer. His sustainable is clearly not mine. He countered my price with sticker shock: seventy-five to a hundred. Maybe it was unfair of me, but I was very unhappy. I soon climbed into my car and drove down to Healdsburg to sit at a bar and meet Kevin and Marcy for a bottle at Scopa. I was overreacting, yet felt kicked in the stomach.

Nevertheless, when I last tasted the Sagrantino in San Francisco, heavy bottle with a flashy price, water addition and all, its vibrancy prevailed. The wine was good, and I was proud.

The U.S. wine industry is a neophyte, with only 150 years of experience. We're still figuring it out—how to grow, where to grow,

how natural is natural, and what to call wines that have the
courage to be naked in farming and in the winery. A country must
start somewhere, and gauging from those embracing the wine
equivalent to slow and thoughtful food, it is clear: We finally have
liftoff.

U.S.-APPROVED ADDITIVES
AND PROCESSES FOR WINE

Acacia (gum arabic)
Acetaldehyde
Activated carbon
Albumen (egg white)
Aluminosilicates (hydrated)
Ammonium phosphate (mono-
and dibasic)
Ascorbic acid isoascorbic acid
(erythorbic acid)
Bentonite (Wyoming clay) and
kaolin
Calcium carbonate
Calcium pantothenate
Calcium sulfate (gypsum)
Carbohydrase (alpha-amylase)
Carbohydrase (beta-amylase)
Carbohydrase (glucoamylase,
amyloglucosidase)
Carbohydrase (pectinase,
cellulase, hemicellulase)
Carbon dioxide (including food-
grade dry ice)

Casein, potassium salt of casein
Catalase
Cellulase
Citric acid
Copper sulfate
Defoaming agents
(polyoxyethylene 40
monostearate, silicon dioxide,
dimethylpolysiloxane,
sorbitan monostearate,
glyceryl mono-oleate, and
glyceryl dioleate)
Dimethyl dicarbonate
Ethyl maltol
Ferrocyanide compounds
(sequestered complexes)
Ferrous sulfate
Fumaric acid
Gelatin (food grade)
Glucose oxidase
Granular cork
Isinglass

Lactic acid
Lysozyme
Malic acid
Malolactic bacteria
Maltol
Milk products (pasteurized
    whole, skim, or half-and-half)
Nitrogen gas
Oak chips or particles,
    uncharred and untreated
Oxygen and compressed air
Pectinase
Polyvinylpyrrolidone (PVPP)
Potassium bitartrate
Potassium carbonate and/or
    potassium bicarbonate
Potassium citrate
Potassium metabisulfite
Protease

Protease (bromelin)
Protease (ficin)
Protease (papain)
Protease (pepsin)
Protease (trypsin)
Silica gel (colloidal silicon
    dioxide)
Sorbic acid and potassium salt
    of sorbic acid
Soy flour (defatted)
Sulfur dioxide
Tannin
Tartaric acid
Thiamine hydrochloride
Urease
Yeast, autolyzed
Yeast, cell wall/membranes of
    autolyzed yeast

CARTE DE MENU: VIN ROUGE
Winemaking at the Eyrie Vineyards in
Twenty-One Simple Steps

This was the "menu" form that David and Jason Lett sent me as an invitation to make a natural wine at their Eyrie Vineyards in Oregon.

Fruit Source
[ ]   Wadenswil clone 1a, Pinot Noir
[ ]   Pommard clone 5, Pinot Noir
[ ]   Dolcetto
[ ]   Pinot Gris

    Rolling Green Fields Vineyard—VSP trellis, elevation 600 feet, yield 2.2 T/A, spacing 6 ↔ 10, planted 1988, own rooted.

Crushing/Stemming
[ ]   Whole cluster
[ ]   Destemmed/whole berries
[ ]   Destemmed/ light crush

Fermenter Type
[ ]   ½ ton food-grade plastic fermenter (Bonnar mfg.)
[ ]   2–3 deheaded barrels

Dry Ice at Stemmer
[ ]   Yes (Alice to arrange the logistics of delivery to the winery.)
[ ]   No

Enzymes
- [ ]   HAH
- [ ]   Color extraction enzymes
- [ ]   Lysozyme

Alice will be responsible for seeing that enzymes do not get carried to other fermenters by cap punchers, pumps, or other tools.

Sulfur Dioxide at Crusher
- [ ]   No SO_2 at crusher
- [ ]   50 ppm SO_2 at crusher
- [ ]   500 ppm SO_2 at crusher (Accad)

Moderate use of SO2 encourages wild Saccharomyces fermentation. No SO2 favors other yeast like Brettanomyces and Candida.

Cold Soak
- [ ]   Yes: Days _____ Fast warm following? _____ (y/n)
- [ ]   No

Yeast Inoculation
- [ ]   Yes. Interval after stemming or cold soak _____
- [ ]   No

Additions
- [ ]   Extractive enzymes
- [ ]   Lysozyme
- [ ]   Enological tannins
- [ ]   Yeast extracts
- [ ]   Oak chips/beans
- [ ]   A lock of Emile Peynaud's hair

Alice will be responsible for preventing inoculation of other fermenters from her designated additions.

Punchdown

[ ]   _____ times per day
[ ]   9" New Zealand plunger
[ ]   *pigeage aux pieds*
[ ]   devise of Alice's own design and construction

Post-Fermentation Maceration

[ ]   Yes
[ ]   No

Pressing

[ ]   Free run only
[ ]   Free run + must pressed with other Eyrie PN
[ ]   Free run + must pressed in cheese cloth by Alice

Barrel

[ ]   2000s
[ ]   1990s
[ ]   1980s
[ ]   1970s

Malolactic Fermentation

[ ]   Yes
[ ]   No

Sulfite Additions Post Malo (2 g *de* SO_2/hl *pour un* pH = 3.6 *ou* 3 g *de* SO_2/hl *pour un* pH = 3.7)

[ ]   Yes
[ ]   No

Eyrie may add sulfites at its discretion if Eyrie perceives a biogenic infection or souring (Brettanomyces, Pediococcus, Acetobacter, etc.) in Alice's barrel that may harm other Eyrie wines.

Fining
[ ]   Yes: Egg? _____ Other? _____
[ ]   No

Racking
[ ]   None prior to bottling
[ ]   One post malo, one prior to bottling

Aging
[ ]   To Sept 2009
[ ]   To Mar 2010

Bottle Type
[ ]   Burgundy heavy
[ ]   Burgundy light

Closure
[ ]   Natural cork 1¾"
[ ]   Natural cork 2"
[ ]   Diam (TCA free, cork-based closure)
[ ]   Glass stopper (if possible)

Foil
[ ]   Standard Eyrie foil
[ ]   Printed paper strip
[ ]   Unfoiled

WINES YOU MIGHT LIKE

This is a short and very personal—and perhaps even eccentric—list of wines that are both natural and natural enough. Some are quirkier than others, and some are just lovely, beautiful wines. Find what you like, who you like, and then buy in every vintage. Tasting a new vintage is another way to learn how your favorite winemakers work. If you have trouble finding them, which is probably the case, search for them on WineSearcher.com.

California
- Coturri Winery (Sonoma)
- Hardesty Cellars (Mendocino)
- Donkey & Goat (Berkeley)
- Natural Process Alliance (Sonoma, local only)
- Arnot-Roberts (Sonoma)
- Clos Saron (Sierra Foothills)
- La Clarine Farm (Sierra Foothills)
- Four Gates (Santa Cruz)
- AmByth Estate (Paso Robles)
- Edmunds St. John (Berkeley)
- Bebame (Berkeley)

Oregon
- Eyrie Vineyards
- Montinore

Finger Lakes, New York
+ Silver Thread

France, by Region
Eastern Loire
+ Du Picatier (Côte Roannaise)
+ Vacheron (Sancerre)
+ Vincent Gaudry (Sancerre)
+ Sebastien Riffault (Sancerre)

Middle Loire
+ Olivier Cousin (Anjou)
+ Sablonettes (Anjou)
+ Pithon-Paillé (Anjou)
+ Domaine de Bellivière (Jasnières and Coteaux du Loir)
+ Domaine le Briseau (Jasnières and Coteaux du Loir)
+ Jean-Pierre Robinot-Les Vignes de l'Angevin (Jasnières and Coteaux du Loir)
+ La Grapperie (Coteaux du Loir)
+ Bernard Baudry (Chinon)
+ Pierre et Catherine Breton (Bourgueil)
+ Clos Roche Blanche (Touraine)
+ Claude Courtois (Sologne)
+ Julien Courtois (Sologne)
+ Vincent Carême (Vouvray)
+ François Pinon (Vouvray)
+ Domaine de Closel (Savennières)
+ Reynald Héaulé (Orleans)
+ Domaine Huet (Vouvay)
+ Chahut et Prodiges (Touraine)
+ Clos de Tue Bouef (Touraine)
+ La Grange Tiphaine (Montlouis su Loire)
+ Thierry Puzelat (Touraine)
+ du Mortier (St-Nicolas de Bourgueil)
+ Noella Morantin (Touraine)
+ Les Vins Contés (Touraine)

- Christian Venier (Cheverny)
- Domaine du Moulin (Cheverny)
- François Cazin (Cheverny)

Western Loire (Sevre et Maine)
- de la Pépière
- Domaines Landron
- Domaine de la Sénéchalière (Marc Pesnot)
- Domaine de l'Ecu (Guy Bossard)

Alsace
- Audrey and Christian Binner
- Pierre Frick
- Gerard Schueller
- Domaine Josmeyer
- Barmes Buecher

Jura
- Philippe Bornard
- Pierre Overnoy/Emmanuel Houillon
- Domaine de la Pinte
- de Montbourgeau
- Jean-François Ganevat

Bugey
- Franck Peillot

Beaujolais
- Marcel Lapierre
- Damien Coquelet
- Domaine Ducroux
- Domaine Foillard
- Louis Claude Desvignes
- Terres Dorées
- Domaine Chamonard

Southern Rhône
+ Eric Texier
+ Domaine de la Gramière
+ Pierre André
+ Domaine de Villeneuve

Norhern Rhône
+ Domaine Romaneaux-Destezet
+ Dard & Ribo
+ Jean & Pierre Gonon
+ Franck Balthazar
+ Thierry Allemand
+ Eric Texier

Provence
+ Andrea Calek (Ardèche)
+ Les Clapas (Ardèche)
+ Domaine de la Tour du Bon
+ Domaine Matassa (Roussilon)

SW and Bordeaux
+ Gombaude-Guillot (Pomerol)
+ Château le Puy (Saint-Emilion et Pomerol)
+ Château Meylet (Saint-Emilion)
+ Le Temps des Cerises (Languedoc)
+ Domaine Deux Anes (Corbieres)
+ Domaine Plageoles (Gaillac)
+ Domaine Mouressipe (Languedoc-Roussillon)
+ Domaine de Souch (Jurançon)

Burgundy
+ Domaine Oudin (Chablis)
+ Alice et Olivier de Moor (Chablis)
+ Philippe Pacalet (Beaune)
+ Michel Lafarge (Volnay)

- ✦ Domaine Prieuré Roch (Vosne-Romanée)
- ✦ Domaine Chandon de Briailles (Savigny-lés-Beaune)
- ✦ Jean-Marie Fourrier (Gevrey-Chambertin)
- ✦ Domaine Giboulot (Beaune)
- ✦ Domaine de Chassorney (Saint-Romain)

Champagne
- ✦ Françoise Bedel
- ✦ Bertrand Gautherot-Vouette et Sorbée
- ✦ Cédric Bouchard
- ✦ Francis Boulard
- ✦ Larmandier-Bernier
- ✦ Champagne David Léclapart
- ✦ Jacques Lassaigne

Italy, by Region
Northern Italy
- ✦ Foradori (Trentino)
- ✦ Ar.Pe.Pe (Valtellina)
- ✦ Vittorio E. Figli Bera (Asti)
- ✦ Az. Agr. Torelli (Asti)
- ✦ Az. Agr. Erbaluna (La Morra)
- ✦ Teobaldo Cappellano (Serralunga d'Alba)
- ✦ Casina Degli Ulivi (Gavi)
- ✦ Camillo Donati Lambrusco (Emilia Romagna)
- ✦ Angelino Maule (Veneto)
- ✦ Costadila Prosecco (Veneto)

Tuscany and Umbria
- ✦ Casina di Cornia (Chianti)
- ✦ La Porta di Vetrine (Chianti)
- ✦ Montesecondo (Chianti)
- ✦ Fontarezza (Montalcino)
- ✦ Stella di Campalto (Montalcino)
- ✦ Giampiero Bea (Umbria)

Sicily
+ Arianna Occhipinti
+ Frank Cornelissen
+ I Vigneri di Salvo Foti

Sardinia
+ Panevino

Spain
+ Mendall (Penedes)
+ Benitos Santos (Rías Baixas)
+ Bodegas Carballo (Las Palmas, Canary Islands)
+ Bodegas Monje (Tenerife, Canary Islands)
+ López de Heredia (Rioja)
+ Els Jelipins (Penedes)
+ Vinos Ambiz (Madrid)

Austria
+ Nikolaihof (Wachau)
+ Hirsch (Kamptal)
+ Jutta Ambrositsch (Vienna)

The Rest of the World
+ Château Musar (Lebanon)
+ Haridimos Hatzidakis (Santorini)
+ Domaine Economou (Crete)
+ Domaine Lucci (Adelaide Hills, Australia)
+ Tom Shobbrook (Adelaide Hills, Australia)
+ Lucy Margaux (Adelaide Hills, Australia)
+ Pheasant's Tears (Republic of Georgia)
+ Jasper Hill (Victoria, Australia)

ACKNOWLEDGMENTS

The road to the book's last drop for this book is paved with my grati-
tude, though it's difficult to grasp where it started. With my mother
who turned me into an ingredient reader at an early age or was it much
later when, in 2000, Joe Dressner, man and importer, pointed out to
me why I was loving certain wines, because they were real ones while
others were over-manipulated. The scene was then set. A few years
down the road, Lisa Donoughe of Watershed Communications made
sure to introduce me to David Lett and his son Jason. We shared what
was for me a very memorable meal in McMinnville and kept the connection going. When Jason invited me to make wine, this particular
journey had its fuel. Once I agreed to play winemaker, Pete Wells, editor of the *New York Times*' dining section, found a place for my story
in the paper, forcing my hand. So a great thank you to Pete as well as
to Mervyn Rothstein, my editor on the *Times*' series they called The
Crush.

My enthusiastic agent, Jane Dystel, stepped on the accelerator when
she uttered three forceful words to me, "Write the proposal." Shortly
thereafter she led me to the absolutely perfect editor, Robert Pigeon
of Da Capo Press. A fascinating man and a great editor. Adding to the
pleasure was his heart-warmingly, endearingly curious palate. He, along
with the team, including Annie Lenth and copy editor Patty Boyd, have
thoughtfully and carefully watched out for me and my words.

When I started to put pen to paper, I headed to Burgundy and to
mentors and muses, Becky Wasserman and Russell Hone. I can never

thank them enough for yet again, and again, offering me food, shelter
and love. Becky even lent me Russell for a wonderful day alone when
he and I sped over to the hills to the Jura, where, after a morel-and-
Savagnin lunch, I had my first meeting ever with the Pierre Overnoy
of Overnoy-Houillon. Overnoy is an icon in this world and the kind
of vigneron who not only humbles me but reminds me why I persist
in writing about this subject. I owe him and the young man he took
under his wing, Emmanuel Houillon, thanks on many levels.

Here's a general shout-out to all who shuttled me, ferried me, cooked
for me, put up with my questions. Specifically, to Thierry Puzelat for
his fabulous honesty and his esprit de joie. To the wine bar genius and
personnage Pierre Jancou who has introduced me to such wonderful
wines and people, including ma fille française, Pascaline. In particular,
thanks to Kevin Hamel, my partner in Sagrantino crime, Ridgely Evers,
who trusted me with his grapes, and the Pellegrini Family Winery for
hosting this project. Thanks to Marcy Mallette for the dinners and the
bedding, and Hank and Caro Beckmeyer for the goats and the road
trip. You loco! José Pastor, whether it is in California or Spain, your
energy and generosity, love you babe.

I am deeply grateful to Laurence Texier for allowing me to kidnap
her husband. Eric was remarkable and tireless in fielding my constant
questions about *piqûre lactique* and carbonic maceration whether in
email, Ten Bells or Charnay. Oh what a pest I must have been. I thank
the Lapierre family for giving me an afternoon; thank you to Marie for
the *asperges*, the warm hugs, and Mathieu for the thoughtfulness. I
thank them all for their Lapierreness. The Chanudets were lovely and
forthcoming, and many thanks to the Foillard's for their time and that
utterly delicious dinner.

Amy and Matt! Scorpion and spider killers! Bon courage for the
Grenache. Thank you for the pick-ups, the shleppings, the friendship,
and Amy I'm so glad you stayed for our magical night with Andrea
Calek, the vignerons and nymphs of Valvigneres. My French publisher
Jean Paul Rocher and his daughter, Marie, not only treated me like
family but gave me terrific context as well and convinced me of the ne-
cessity of visiting Jacques Néauport. Which brings me to Jacques and
mothers. Jacques picking me chanterelles was a generosity and treat I'll

always remember, my interview with him was essential, and I was so happy he was willing to meet with me. He also has a wonderful mother, Ginette, who slaved for days over the stove and delivered what was the marathon meal of my life. *To ma fille Française*, Pascaline Lepeltier, the best "daughter" a mother could have. And as far as my own mother, Ethel, while she prefers Matuk rouge soft to whole cluster Gamay, she has always been in my corner, and never fails to give me good copy.

Jenny Lefcourt always found a seat in her car for me during January tasting marathons, beds at Domaine Deux Anes, and at Olivier Cousin (thank you, Magali, Dominique, Olivier, and Claire), and an ear for me in New York City at any time. Another thank you to Rail Europe. This company was kindly supportive, extending train passes so I could more easily do my research. It was extremely helpful and a special thanks to Samina. From the bottom of my heart, a thank you to Kathryn and Loren Lieberthal for their generous and unbidden "travel grant," a gift that left me breathless and embarrassed, and extremely touched (and it was swiftly put to excellent use!).

Writing is often such a lonely task, which makes friends like Kathryn and Loren all the more cherished. That I have others makes me very fortunate; among them, Frank Bruni. A great big smooch for his continued guidance and that reaction to Patapon, a true seed that germinated in this book. I hope I have not worn out my welcome with other members of my cheering squad. I rely on them far too often. One of them is my friend and best travel buddy, Melissa Clark, who is always there with love, advice, recipes, and shortbread.

Elizabeth Minchilli and Nancy Trent always encourage me when I'm feeling down and are equipped with the best pep talks in just the right tone. Thanks to Nancy for Trent & Company's support and one special nod to Walter Sperr for his extra set of eyes at the last minute. Liz Reisberg, a great friend and for years, has been my secret weapon when it comes to grammar and syntax before I let anyone else see it.

My Thursday night core pillars are Hilary Davidson, Amy Klein, Tony Powell, Kate Walter, Royal Young, and Rich Prior. A special big kiss to Sue Shapiro for inviting me into our writing group in the first place. A stellar friend and colleague and critic; her insightful comments always spot-on.

Aurore Besson in Paris and Stephen diRenza in Fes took time from their days to give me general reading notes. Thanks to the inspirational Jancis Robinson for delivering the news that I was official runner up for the Geoffrey Roberts Award, which was a sweet pat on the back, and a bit of applause for my writing.

Finally, another thank you to two men I knew very briefly but whose influence will remain great. My book opened with David Lett's death. Twenty-four months later, almost as I wrote my last words, Marcel Lapierre died. The coincidence was unnerving yet poignant. I hope I have done them justice in writing this book. A final thank you to them and to their family who will carry on and make the wine world a better place, inspiring more vignerons to make the connection between agriculture, grape, man, and magic.

INDEX

Note: AF refers to Alice Feiring.